DICTIONARY OF
1000
CHINESE PROVERBS

DICTIONARY OF
1000
CHINESE PROVERBS

Translated and Edited by
Marjorie Lin and Schalk Leonard

HIPPOCRENE BOOKS
New York

Copyright © 1998 by Hippocrene Books
All rights reserved.

For information, address:
HIPPOCRENE BOOKS
171 Madison Avenue
New York, NY 10016

ISBN 0-7818-0682-8

Cataloging-in-Publication Data available from the Library of Congress.

Dictionary of 1000 Chinese proverbs with English equivalents /
Translated and edited by Marjorie Lin and Schalk Leonard.
p.   cm.
Includes bibliographical references and index.
1. Proverbs, Chinese. 2. English language--Dictionaries--Chinese.
3. Chinese language--Dictionaries--English. I. Lin, Marjorie.
II. Leonard, Schalk.
PN6519.C5D53   1998   98-7813
398.9'951'03--dc21   CIP

Printed in the United States of America.

Introduction

Selection of 1,000 Chinese Proverbs

The authors have assembled in this volume one thousand of the most "significant" proverbs found in the Chinese language. For each proverb selected, there exists in the Chinese literary and oral tradition many others that could not be included. Fundamental consideration in the selection process was given to the possibility that the dictionary will be used by different groups of individuals with different aims. It is the intent of the authors that this work will be of simultaneous value to the English language speaker interested in Chinese proverbs and their wisdom, the English language speaker interested in Chinese proverbs as a tool for Chinese language study, and the Chinese language speaker who might use the translations as a tool for English language study.

Significance, as the central criterion of selection, includes frequency of use, but also refers to the tendency of the proverb to express traditional Chinese wisdom, beliefs, values, and aspirations. In this volume may be found proverbs that express Taoist and Buddhist truths, Confucian rules of propriety, admonishments from the elderly, exhortations from parents, and advice from teachers. The reader may discover, after a generous perusal of the Chinese proverbs contained herein, certain unique and traditional features of Chinese life and thought. Among those features one may note a strong preference for the particular over the general and the concrete over the abstract, frequent use of symbolism, respect for the wisdom of the ancients, an emphasis on study and learning, a tendency toward caution and frugality, strong esteem for hierarchy, reliance on individual ethics, and a search for truth through study of nature.

The Chinese Language and Organization of the Dictionary

The main body of the dictionary contains the following elements: a Chinese language key word for each entry (using the pinyin romanization of the Mandarin dialect term), a sequential number from one to one thousand, a pinyin romanization spelling of the Chinese proverb, and an English translation of the proverb.

The Chinese language, a branch of the Sino-Tibetan language family, includes seven major dialects. In this work, the Mandarin dialect (referred to in Chinese as 'putonghua') is used exclusively. Chinese-Mandarin is said to be the oldest continuously spoken language on earth, claims more speakers than any other language on earth, and is by far the most widely used and understood dialect of Chinese.

The use of key words allows for an alphabetical listing of the proverbs. In selecting a key word, primary consideration was given to the single word in the Chinese proverb central to the proverb's meaning and significance. In many cases, the key word is the first word of a Chinese language compound word made up of normally two words. In those cases, rather than list the full compound word, only the first word is used. This more accurately reflects the monosyllabic nature of the Chinese language and is consistent with the traditional organization of a Chinese language dictionary.

The pinyin system of romanization is used throughout the dictionary (except in the bibliography, where long established alternate romanization methods are used for certain terms). The pinyin system was established in the People's Republic of China in the 1950s and has gained increasing acceptance throughout the world as the standard romanization system for the Chinese language.

Regarding translation of the proverbs, preference was given to fidelity to the original Chinese expression. In certain cases, however, well-established English proverbs are provided, alone or in addition to a more literal translation of the proverb. In many of these cases, the

Chinese proverb could not be translated literally in a meaningful way due to the archaic construction or condensed nature of the classical phrase.

At the end of the dictionary, an alternative method of locating a given proverb is provided through the use of an English language key word index. Here, the vast majority of the English key words are literal translations of their Chinese counterpoints. However, as with translation of the proverbs, in certain cases, literal translations were impossible. In such cases, English key words were selected from the English phrase using the same criteria as was used in selecting a Chinese language key word for the phrase.

Finally, an appendix has been provided with each Chinese proverb written in Chinese characters and listed in the same order as the proverbs in the main body of the dictionary. The Chinese language, as used by the Chinese, is a language of speech and written characters, absent romanization features. Inclusion of the character appendix will allow the Chinese language speaker to understand with certainty each term of the Chinese proverb, while providing the English speaking student of the Chinese language a tool for accessing each word in a Chinese language dictionary and exploring additional meanings and uses.

A

Ai	1	Ai mo da yu xin si. There is no greater sorrow than a frozen heart.
	2	Ai wu ji wu. Love me, love my dog.
	3	Ai yao xi shui chang liu. Love me little, love me long.
	4	Xi hua hua jie guo, ai liu liu cheng yin. Love and attention make all things grow.
An	5	Ju an si wei. In times of peace, do not forget danger.
Ao	6	Jiao ao shi sheng li de di ren. Arrogance is the enemy of victory.

B

Ba	7	Yi ge ba zhang pai bu xiang. A single hand cannot clap. It takes two to make a quarrel.

Ba   7   Yi ge ba zhang pai bu xiang.
                        A single hand cannot clap.
                        It takes two to make a quarrel.

Bai   8   Dong jia bu bai luo, xi jia bu fa zuo.
                        If Peter doesn't fail, Paul doesn't prosper.

Ban   9   Xing yao hao ban, zhu yao hao lin.
                        For a trip, choose good companions;
                        for a home, choose good neighbors.

Bao   10   Bao han bu zhi e han ji.
                        The well-fed don't know how the starving
                        suffer.

                11   Bao si liu pi, ren si liu ming.
                        The leopard dies but leaves his skin;
                        a man dies but leaves his reputation.

                12   Lin she hao, wu jia bao.
                        A good neighbor is a priceless treasure.

                13   Shan e dao tou zhong you bao;
                        yuan zou gao fei ye nan tiao.
                        Good and bad ultimately lead to
                        inescapable consequences.

14 Shan you shan bao, e you e bao.
Good has its reward, and evil has its cost.

15 Yi qiu wu jia bao, nan de you qing lang.
It's easier to find a priceless treasure
than to find an affectionate man.

Bei 16 Bei ru bei chu.
Ill-gotten, ill-spent. Easy come, easy go.

17 Deng gao bi zi bei.
The road to high places begins in low places.

Bi 18 Ren bi ren, qi si ren.
Comparisons are odious.

Bian 19 Bian dan mei za, liang tou da ta.
When the shoulder pole is not secured at both
ends, the load will slip off.

20 Ku hai wu bian, hui tou shi an.
The sea of bitterness has no bounds -
repent and the shore is near.

21 Qi shi er bian, ben xiang nan bian.
Of the seventy two kinds of change, changing
original nature is the most difficult.

22 Xiong bian shi yin, chen mo shi jin.
Eloquence is silver, silence is golden.

Bie 23 Xiao bie sheng xin hun.
Reunion after a brief separation is better than
a honeymoon.

Bing	24	Ai bing bi sheng. An army burning with righteous indignation is bound to win.
	25	Bing bu li zhen, hu bu li shan. Soldiers don't stray from their posts; tigers don't stray from the mountain.
	26	Bing bu yan zha. All is fair in war.
	27	Bing cong kou ru, huo cong kou chu. The mouth is the entry point of disease and the departure point for misfortune.
	28	Bing dong san chi, fei yi ri zhi han. It takes more than one cold day for a river to freeze three feet deep. Big problems do not emerge overnight.
	29	Bing gui jing, bu gui duo. Troops are valued for their quality, not for their quantity.
	30	Bing gui shen su, ren gui si suo. Troops are valued for their speed, as men are valued for their minds.
	31	Bing hao bu xie yi, xia ci mei ren yi. Thank the doctor when you recover, or you won't find a doctor the next time you are ill.
	32	Bing ji luan tou yi. Try any doctor when critically ill. Try anything in a desperate situation.

33   Bing sui jiang xiang cao sui feng.
Troops follow their general as grass follows the
wind.

34   Ji bing zai zhi, man bing zai yan.
An emergency illness requires treatment;
a chronic illness requires recuperation.

35   Jiao bing bi bai.
An army puffed up with pride is bound to
lose.

36   Jiu bing cheng liang yi.
Prolonged illness makes a doctor of a patient.

37   Jiu bing wu xiao zi.
There are no filial children at the bedside of
chronically ill parents.

38   Tong bing xiang lian.
Those who have the same illness sympathize
with each other.

39   Yang bing qian ri, yong bing yi shi.
Troops are trained long, but are
expended in a moment.

40   You bing cai zhi jian shi xian.
Health is not valued until illness comes.

41   You bing zao zhi, sheng qian sheng shi.
Tend to an illness early, and save both
money and effort.

C

Cai

42   Cai duo bu lu, yi gao bu xian,
ai lu ai xian, bi you feng xian.
Don't parade your riches or talent;
those who show off court danger.

43   Cai duo lei shen, yu duo shang shen.
Excess money tires the body, excess
desire harms the soul.

44   Cai duo zhao zei, ren jun zhao xie.
Wealth attracts thieves, as beauty attracts evil.

45   Mai le pian yi cai, shao lan jia di guo.
Buy cheap wood and you'll burn your pot.

46   Qin sui qin, cai bo fen.
Keep your money separate, even from
family members.

47   Qing cai nan shao, jiao zi nan jiao.
Green wood is hard to burn, and a
pampered child is hard to teach.

48   Ren wei cai si, niao wei shi wang.
Man dies for money, birds die for food.

	49	Tian sheng wo cai bi you yong. Every life has a purpose.
	50	Wu tan yi wai zhi cai. Don't covet unexpected fortune.
	51	Xiao cai bu chu, da cai bu ru. You must invest a little to gain a lot.
Cang	52	Ceng jing cang hai nan wei shui. To the sophisticated person, there's nothing new under the sun.
Cao	53	Cao xin yi lao. Worry causes aging.
Ce	54	San shi liu ce, zou wei shang ce. He that fights and runs away may live to fight another day.
Cha	55	Cha zhi hao li, miu yi qian li. One false move may lead to major defeat. The slightest deviance may lead one far astray.
	56	Hao cha bu pa xi pin, hao shi bu pa xi lun. Good tea will stand up to a taste test, and good deeds will stand up to examination.
	57	Ning he peng you de dan cha, bu he di ren de mi jiu. Better to drink the weak tea of a friend than the sweet wine of an enemy.
Chan	58	You heng chan, bu ru you heng xin. Perseverance is worth more than a vast estate.

Chang	59	Chang shuo kou li shun, chang zuo shou bu ben. Practice makes perfect.
	60	Qu ren zhi chang, bu ji zhi duan. Overcome one's weaknesses by learning from other's strengths.
Chao	61	Fu chao zhi xia wu wan luan. When the nest is overturned, all eggs will be broken.
Che	62	Che dao shan qian bi you lu. The cart will find its way around the hill when it gets there. Things will work out in time.
	63	Qian che zhi fu, hou che zhi jian. The overturned cart up ahead serves as a warning to the carts behind. Take heed of another man's mistake.
Cheng	64	Bu pa xue bu cheng, jiu pa xin bu cheng. Be more concerned about the sincerity of your effort than about your ability to learn.
	65	Cheng gong shi san fen tian cai qi fen nu li. Success is three parts genius and seven parts hard work.
	66	Jing cheng suo zhi, jin shi wei kai. No difficulty is insurmountable if one is determined.
	67	Qiao zha bu ru jue cheng. Honesty is the best policy.

68 Yi ren nan cheng bai ren yi.
You can't please all of the people all of the
time.

Chi 69 Chi kui jiu shi zhan pian yi.
The lesson you learn when you are
taken advantage of puts you at an advantage.

70 Huo wen san jia bu chi kui.
Shop around and you'll never get cheated.

Chou 71 Chou ren ai dai hua.
Ugly people like to wear fancy adornments.

72 Chou ren ai zuo guai.
Ugly people like to do outrageous things.

73 Fu qi chao zui bu ji chou.
Spouses quarrel without holding a grudge.

74 Jia chou be ke wai yang.
Don't wash your dirty laundry in public.

75 Liu shui bu chou, chou shui bu liu.
Flowing water doesn't stink, and stinky
water doesn't flow.

76 Ren si bu ji chou.
A dead man bears no grudges.

77 Tian tian bu fa chou, huo dao bai chu tou.
Avoid worry each day and live to a ripe old
age.

78 Wu chou bu cheng xi.
Every drama requires a fool.

79   Yi zui jie qian chou, xing hou hai zai chou.
      Drink drowns your sorrow, but your sorrow
      returns the morning after.

Chu   80   Chu zi duo pang zi.
                 Cooks are generally plump.

81   Yang mao chu zai yang shen shang.
      In the long run, whatever you're given you
      pay for.

Chuan   82   Bai chuan gui hai.
                   All rivers return to the sea. All roads lead to
                   Rome.

83   Chuan da chi shui shen.
      Large boats have a deep draft.

84   Chuan dao jiang xin bu lou chi.
      It's too late to plug the leak when the boat is in
      mid-stream.

85   Hou shang chuan zhe xian shang an.
      The last to board is the first to debark.

86   Xiao chuan bu yi zhong zai.
      Small boats shouldn't carry large loads.

Chuang   87   Chang kai chuang, bao jian kang.
                    Open the window and improve your health.

Ci   88   Ci bu zhang bing, yi bu zhang cai.
                The merciful do not engage in war,
                and the righteous do not engage in finances.

Cong	89	Cong ming bao yi ren, fu gui bao yi jia. Intelligence provides for the individual, riches provide for the whole family.
	90	Cong ming fan bei cong ming wu. Clever people may be victims of their own cleverness.
	91	Cong ming ren ye hui zuo sa shi. Smart people also do stupid things.
Cu	92	Cu shi chen de suan. Vinegar grows more pungent with age.
Cuo	93	Wei ren bu pa cuo, jiu pa bu gai guo. Fear not mistakes, but fear repeating them.

D

Da   94   Bu da bu cheng qi.
Spare the rod and spoil the child.

95   Bu da bu xiang shi.
No discord, no concord.

96   Da shi teng, ma shi ai.
Discipline springs from love.

Dan   97   Bu tiao dan zi bu zhi zhong;
bu zou chang lu bu zhi yuan.
You can't appreciate the weight until you
shoulder the load; you can't appreciate the
length of a road until you travel it.

98   Dan xiao zuo be de jiang jun.
The timid cannot become generals.

99   Kan ren tiao dan bu chi li.
The load carried by another does not seem so
heavy.

100   Zheng dan hao tiao, pian dan nan ai.
The pole is easy to carry if the load is balanced.

Dang   101   Bu shang dang, bu cheng nei hang.
If you have never been fooled, you'll never
become an expert.

102   Tou hui shang dang, er hui xin liang.
Once bitten, twice shy.

Dao   103   Dao qiang bu ren ren.
Weapons make no distinctions among men.

104   De dao duo zhu, shi dao gua zhu.
A just cause will enjoy abundant support,
while an unjust cause will find little support.

105   Fang xia tu dao, li di cheng fou.
A butcher becomes a Buddha the moment he
drops his cleaver.

106   Jun zi mou dao bu mou shi.
Righteous men seek truth, not food.

107   Ye dao hen ming yue.
Thieves in the dark hate the moonlight.

108   Yi ren de dao, ji quan sheng tian.
When a man gets to the top, his friends and
relatives accompany him.

De   109   De bu zu xi, shi bu zu you.
One should not be happy about a gain
or despondent about a loss.

110   Shang de bu de, shi yi you de.
A truly good man is not aware of his goodness,
and therefore, he is good.

Di   111   Huang he you di, ren xin wu di.
There is a bottom to the Huang River, but
none to the human heart.

112   Juan juan zhi di, hui cheng jiang he.
A great river is the result of many little drops.

113   Qian li zhi di, kui yu yi xue.
A single ant hole may lead to the collapse
of an enormous dike.

Die   114   Zi ji die dao zi ji pa.
If you fall down by yourself, get up by
yourself.

Dong   115   Bu jing dong han, na zhi chun nuan.
You must live through winter to appreciate the
warmth of spring.

116   Dong bu jie yue chun yao chou,
xia bu lao dong qiu wu shou.
Be thrifty in winter or you'll have worries
in the spring; be industrious in the summer
or you'll have no harvest in the autumn.

117   Long dong zhi hou, bi you yang chun.
After a heavy winter comes a sunny spring.

Du   118   Bu du shi ying qian.
You win by not gambling.

119   Chu sheng zhi du bu wei hu.
New-born calves have no fear of tigers.

120   Ge ceng du pi ge chong shan.
You can never really fathom the mind of
another.

E

121 E bu ji, bu zu yi shang shen.
If you don't do bad deeds, you will not harm
yourself.

122 E ren xian gao zhuang.
The guilty party is the first to sue.

123 Ji e zhe sang.
Those who accumulate bad deeds will lose.

124 Wan e jie you zi si qi.
Selfishness is the root of all evil.

125 Yi ren zuo e, qian ren zao yang.
When one person performs a bad act,
one thousand people suffer.

126 Yao zhi fu mu en, huai li bao er sun.
You will understand a parent's love
when you hold your own child in your arms.

127 Yi ye fu qi bai ri en.
One evening as husband and wife -
one hundred evenings of kindness.

Er

128 Ai er dang xun zi.
If you love your child,
you should discipline your child.

129 Er bu xian mu chou, gou bu xian zhu pin.
A child will never desert its mother
though she may be homely; a dog will never
forsake its master though he may be poor.

130 Er da bu you ye, nu da bu you niang.
When boys grow up, they are beyond
the father's control; when girls grow up,
they are beyond the mother's control.

131 Er xing qian li mu dan you.
When the child takes a trip,
the mother will worry.

132 Xiao er wu zha bing.
Small children do not deceive.

133 Yi er hao du, zhong mu nan yan.
You can plug one person's ears,
but you can't close everyone's eyes.

F

Fa 134 Wang zi fan fa, yu min tong zui.
When the prince breaks the law, he should be
punished like everyone else.

Fan 135 An ren kou zuo fan, liang shen ti cai yi.
Cut your coat according to your cloth.

136 Fan hou bai bu zou, huo dao jiu shi jiu.
A walk after a meal makes for a long life.

137 Fan mo bu jiao bian tun,
hua mo bu xiang jiu shuo.
Do not swallow your food without chewing,
and do not speak without thinking.

138 Fan nao bu xun ren, ren zi xun fan nao.
Worry doesn't seek out people -
people find worry on their own.

139 Fan shi qi tou nan, zuo le jiu bu nan.
Everything is difficult at the beginning;
but once done, nothing is difficult.

140 Jin ri qie chi jin ri fan, ming tian you shi,
ming tian ban.
Eat today's food today; take care of
tomorrow's work tomorrow.

141 Leng zhou leng fan hao chi,
leng yan leng yu nan shou.
A cold meal is acceptable - not so sarcastic
comments.

142 Ning ke chi cuo fan, bu ke shuo cuo hua.
Better to eat the wrong food than say the
wrong words.

Fang 143 Xiang yang fang zi xian de nuan,
kao shui ren jia hui cheng chuan.
The house that faces the sun warms up first;
the person that lives near water knows how
to row a boat.

144 Yu ren fang bian, zi ji fang bian.
Do someone a favor and you do yourself a
favor.

Feng 145 Bai li bu tong feng.
Every one hundred miles you'll find different
customs.

146 Feng ren zhi shuo san fen hua.
Maintain your reserve when in discourse with
others.

147 Ji feng zhi jing cao.
The force of the wind tests the strength of the
grass.

148 Ni feng dian huo zi shao shen.
Light a fire in the face of the wind and you
will burn yourself.

149 San nian feng shui lun liu zhuan.
Every dog has his day.

150 Shan yu yu lai feng man lou.
A turbulent wind precedes the mountain
storm.

151 Shun feng chui huo, yong li bu duo.
Blow on the fire with the wind at your back
and you'll expend less effort.

152 Wu feng bu qi lang.
Where there's smoke, there's fire.

Fu

153 Chou fu jia zhong bao.
The ugly housewife is a treasure at home.

154 Da fu you tian, xiao fu you jian.
Great wealth is a gift from heaven,
moderate wealth results from frugality.

155 Da zhang fu neng qu neng shen.
The true man should be able to both yield and
stand firm.

156 Fu chang fu sui.
Husband sings a song, wife sings along.

157 Fu gui hao, bu ru er sun hao.
Good offspring are better than material wealth.

158 Fu wu shuang zhi.
Blessings never come in pairs.

159 Hu fu wu quan zi.
A tiger father will not produce a dog son.

160 Huo fu wei lin.
Fortune and misfortune are neighbors.

161 Huo xi fu suo yi, fu xi huo suo fu.
Good fortune lies within bad; bad fortune
lurks within good.

162 Pin jian fu qi bai shi ai.
Life is filled with sorrow for a poor couple.

163 Qiao fu nan wei wu mi zhi chui.
Even the cleverest housewife cannot cook a
meal without rice. You can't make something
out of nothing.

164 Rao ren shi fu.
A pardon produces good fortune.

165 Sai weng shi ma, yan zhi fei fu.
When the old frontiersman lost his horse,
who could have guessed it was a blessing
in disguise? A loss may turn out to be a gain.

166 Shen zai fu zhong bu zhi fu.
When we are happy, we aren't aware we are
happy.

167 Tian xia wu bu shi de fu mu.
No parent is ever wrong.

168 Yi fen du liang yi fen fu,
neng ren bian shi you fu ren.
An ounce of tolerance, an ounce of good
fortune.

169   Yong ren duo hou fu.
       Fortune favors fools.

170   You qi fu, bi you qi zi.
       Like father, like son.

G

Gen   171   Duo shen de gen ji, zhu duo gao de qiang.
The depth of the foundation determines
the height of the wall.

172   Shu kao gen, wu kao liang.
As roots are essential for a tree, beams are
essential for a house.

173   Zhan cao bu chu gen, chun feng
chui you sheng.
If you don't kill the root, the problem will
return.

Gong   174   Gong dao zi ran cheng.
Constant effort yields certain success.

175   Gong yu shan qi shi, bi xian li qi qi.
A workman must first sharpen his tools
if he is to do his work well.

176   Hao dou de gong ji bu zhang mao.
The cock that loves a fight grows no hair.

177   Kai gong mei you hui tou jian.
The arrow once released cannot be retrieved.
What is done cannot be undone.

178 Man gong chu xi huo.
Steady application makes a superior product.

179 Wu gong bu shou lu.
No reward without good deeds.

180 Yi ri du shu yi ri gong, yi ri bu du shi ri kong.
A day of reading is a day of gain; a day without
reading is ten days of loss.

181 Zuo shi bu yi zhong, lei si ye wu gong.
No matter how hard you work, you'll get no
credit if you don't follow the local practice.

Gou

182 Da gou kan zhu ren.
Know the status of the master before you beat
the dog.

183 Da gou pa qiang, xiao gou kan yang.
Monkey see, monkey do.

184 Gou ji tiao qiang.
When cornered, a dog will jump over the wall.

185 Hao gou bu dang dao.
A good dog won't get in the way.

186 Hao gou bu yao ji, hao han bu da qi.
A good dog won't attack the chickens,
and a good man won't beat his wife.

187 Hui jiao de gou bu hui yao ren.
A barking dog seldom bites.

188 Lao gou xue bu lai xin hua yang.
You cannot teach an old dog new tricks.

189   Tian qing bu kai gou, yu luo pian di liu.
       Dig a ditch while the sky is clear,
       or you'll have a flood when it rains.
       Make hay while the sun shines.

190   Yao ren gou, bu lou chi.
       The dog that bites won't bare his teeth.

Gu   191   De bu gu, bi you lin.
       No man is an island.

192   Gu bu qiao bu xiang, li bu bian bu ming.
       Strike a drum to make a sound;
       debate the truth for it to become evident.

193   Gu kong ze sheng gao, ren kuang ze hua da.
       Empty drums make loud noise;
       arrogant men make loud boasts.

Gua   194   Gua fu men qian shi fei duo.
       There are many disputes in front of
       the widow's door.

195   Gua jiu nan he, gua fu nan ao.
       It's no fun to drink alone, and it's hard being a
       widow.

196   Zhong gua de gua, zhong dou de dou.
       As you sow, so shall you reap.

Guai   197   Jian guai bu guai, qi guai zi bai.
       Ghosts exist only for those who believe in
       them.

Guan   198   Da le san nian guan si, dang de ban ge lu shi.
       Pursue a lawsuit for three years, and you'll
       know almost as much as a lawyer.

199 Qing guan nan duan jia wu shi.
Even the best judge cannot settle a domestic
dispute.

200 Wu guan yi shen qing.
Avoid officialdom, and your life will be easy.

201 Xin guan bu guan jiu shi.
Newly appointed officials don't handle old
business.

202 Xin guan shang ren san ba huo.
A new broom sweeps clean.

Guang   203 Guang yin rong yi guo, sui yue mo cuo tuo.
Time passes quickly - don't waste it.

204 Guang yin ru liu shui, yi qu bu fu hui.
Time is like a river - it flows by
and doesn't return.

205 Guang yin si jian.
Time flies like an arrow.

206 Yi cun guang yin yi cun jin,
cun jin nan mai cun guang yin.
A moment of time is like a piece of gold,
but a piece of gold won't buy a moment of
time.

Gui   207 Gui ren duo wang shi.
Distinguished persons are apt to be forgetful.

Guo   208 Chang si ji guo, mian yu zhao huo.
Ponder your faults and you will avert
misfortune.

209   Guo er bu gai, shi wei guo yi.
It's a mistake to make a mistake
and not correct it.

210   Guo er neng gai, shan mo da yan.
The ability to correct a mistake
is a wonderful thing.

211   Guo jia xing wang, pi fu you ze.
Every man has a share of responsibility
for the fate of his country.

212   Guo yi min wei ben, min yi shi wei tian.
The people are the foundation of the state,
and food is vital to the people.

213   Guo you bu ji.
Going beyond is as bad as falling short.

214   Guo zhi ben zai jia, jia zhi ben zai shen.
The foundation of a nation is the family,
and the foundation of a family is the
individual.

215   Mai guo yao qiao da, qu jia yao xi cha.
When buying a pot, bang it first;
when marrying, make thorough inquiries first.

H

Ha   216   Ha ma you shi ye hui bei ni xian zhu.
                   Even frogs sometimes get stuck in the mud.

Hai   217   Hai shui bu ke dou liang.
                   The sea cannot be measured with a bushel.
                   Great minds cannot be fathomed
                   by ordinary minds.

            218   Qiong ren de hai zi zao dang jia.
                   Children of poor families take charge of the
                   household at an early age.

            219   Si hai zhi nei jie xiong di.
                   All men are brothers.

            220   You ma de hai zi xiang ge bao,
                   mei niang de hai zi xiang gen cao.
                   A child with a mother is like a treasure;
                   a child without a mother is like a lone
                   blade of grass.

Han   221   Hao han bu chi yan qian kui.
                   A true man doesn't fight against
                   impossible odds.

222 Hao han zuo shi hao han dang.
A true man takes responsibility for his actions.

223 Nan zi han da zhang fu,
bu wei wu dou mi zhe yao.
The true man will not compromise his
principles for a meager reward.

224 Ruo fei yi fan han che gu,
yan de mei hua pu bi xiang.
Without the bitter cold of winter,
how can one enjoy the fragrance of
the plum blossoms?

Hang 225 Hang hang chu zhuang yan.
Every trade has the potential for mastery.

226 Hang hang you li, hang hang you bi.
There are pros and cons in every line of work.

227 Nan pa ru cuo hang, nu pa jia cuo lang.
Men worry about entering the wrong trade,
women worry about marrying the wrong man.

228 Tong hang shi yuan jia.
Those in the same trade contend with each
other.

229 Tong hang xiang ji.
Two of a trade can never agree.

230 Zuo yi hang, yuan yi hang,
dao lao bu zai hang.
Grumble about your job and you'll be good at
nothing when you get old.

Hao   231   Hao ren bu chang shou, huai ren huo bai nian.
              The good die young and the evil live to one
              hundred.

          232   Hao shi bu guo san.
              Fortune knocks but thrice.

          233   Hao shi duo mo.
              The road to happiness is filled with setbacks.

He   234   Guang tou bu yi ding shi he shang.
              Not every bald head belongs to a monk.

          235   He li yan si hui shui ren.
              Swimmers will die by drowning.
              Live by the sword, die by the sword.

          236   He qi sheng cai.
              The good-natured person will likely get rich.

          237   He you liang an, shi you liang mian.
              Rivers have two banks, and every issue has two
              sides.

          238   Jia he wan shi xing.
              If the family lives in harmony, all affairs will
              prosper.

          239   Lan he shang zuo bu chu hao zhai lai.
              Lazy monks don't prepare tasty meals.

          240   Wai lai de he shang hui nian jing.
              Monks from abroad recite the scriptures better.

          241   Xiao he gou ye neng fan chuan.
              Even a small stream can tip a boat.

242 Yao xiang guo he xian da qiao.
If you want to cross the river, you must first
build a bridge.

243 Yi ge he shang tiao shui he,
liang ge he shang tai shui he,
san ge he shang mei shui he.
One monk carries water to drink,
two monks lug water to drink, and
three monks will have no water to drink.
Too many cooks spoil the soup.

244 Zuo yi ri he shang, zhuang yi ri zhong.
If you're a monk for a day, toll the bell for a
day. Carry out the duties of your station.

Heng 245 Ren you heng xin wan shi cheng.
Perseverance will guarantee success.

Hu 246 Hu du bu shi zi.
Even a vicious tiger will not eat its offspring.

247 Hua hu hua pi nan hua gu,
zhi ren zhi mian bu zhi xin.
In drawing a tiger you draw the skin
but not the bones; knowing a man,
you know his face but not his heart.

248 Lao hu ye you da kun shi.
Even the tiger dozes off. No one is perfect.

249 Liang hu xiang zheng, bi you yi shang.
When two tigers do battle, one will get hurt.
Diamond cuts diamond.

250　Shang shan qin hu yi, kai kou qiu ren nan.
It's easier to catch a tiger on a mountain than to beg for help.

251　Duo chi wu zi wei, duo hua bu zhi qian.
A glut of food is tasteless, a glut of words is worthless.

252　Fang hua nan ru yuan er duo.
Square words won't fit into a round ear.

253　Hao hua san bian, lian gou dou xian.
Even dogs get tired of hearing the same praise over and over again.

254　Hao kan de hua er wei bi xiang.
Pretty flowers are not necessarily fragrant.

255　Hua bu tou ji ban ju duo.
When a conversation turns nasty, to say one word more is a waste of breath.

256　Hua bu yao shuo si, lu bu yao zou jue.
Do not issue ultimatums and do not travel down the road of no return.

257　Hua duo bu tian, jiao duo bu nian.
An overabundance of words is unpleasant; an overabundance of glue is not sticky.

258　Hua duo le shang ren, shi duo le shang shen.
Too much talk harms a person, and too much food harms the body.

259   Hua mei mei yi shi, ren mei mei yi shi.
A flower's beauty is fleeting; a person's beauty a lifetime.

260   Hua you chong kai ri, ren wu zai shao nian.
Flowers may bloom again, but man never recaptures his youth.

261   Kan hua rong yi xiu hua nan.
It is easy to view a flower, but difficult to embroider one.

262   Lao hu hua zai bei, ren xin hua zai nei.
A tiger's pattern is on his back and a person's machinations are in his heart.

263   Ting xiao hua, wu da shi.
Listen to idle talk and doom great plans.

Huo   264   Bu gui nan de zhi huo, shi min bu wei dao.
Not collecting treasures prevents stealing.

265   Bu tan cai, huo bu lai.
He who knows when enough is enough will not encounter misfortune.

266   Chuang huo rong yi xiao zai nan.
It is easy to court trouble, but hard to avert it.

267   Gai de zhu huo, cang bu zhu yan.
You can cover up fire, but you can't hide smoke.

268   Hao huo bu pa shi, pa shi mei hao huo.
Quality merchandise can stand up to a test; otherwise, it is not quality merchandise.

269 Hao huo bu pian yi, pian yi wu hao huo.
Quality merchandise is not cheap, and cheap
things are not quality merchandise.

270 Huo bu dan xing.
Misfortune never comes alone.

271 Huo fu wu men, wei ren zi zhao.
There are no doors leading to fortune or
misfortune - your actions will determine which
one you court.

272 Huo fu zi qu.
We make or break ourselves.

273 Huo ji lao bu hao bing,
huo meng shao bu hao fan.
Too much heat destroys the food.

274 Huo nan ru shen jia zhi men.
Misfortune does not easily enter the home of
the cautious man.

275 Kui ren shi huo.
It is misfortune to treat people unfairly.

276 Lian tie xu yao lie huo,
jiao you xu yao cheng xin.
Forging iron requires great heat;
making friends requires sincerity.

277 Lie huo jian chun jin.
Genius gold fears no fire.

278 Xing xing zhi huo ke yi liao yuan.
A single spark can start a prairie fire.

279 Ye huo shao bu jin, chuan feng chui you sheng.
Not even a prairie fire can destroy the grass;
it grows back when the spring breeze blows.

J

280   Bu chi fan ze ji, bu du shu ze yu.
      Eat to ward off starvation; study to ward off
      ignorance.

281   Da ji bu shi xi mi.
      Large roosters don't eat fine rice.

282   Hao ji xing bu ru lan bi tou.
      A strong memory is not as good as a marginal
      written record.

283   Huang shu lang gei ji bai nian, mei an hao xin.
      The weasel goes to pay his respects on the hen
      with less than the best of intentions.

284   Ji bu ze shi.
      A starving man is not picky about his food.
      Beggars can't be choosers.

285   Ji du na zhi ya du.
      How can a chicken understand how a duck
      thinks?

286   Ji fei bu xia dan.
      Plump hens lay no eggs.

287 Ji si cheng lu, ji cun cheng chi.
Many a little makes a mickle.

288 Jian ji xing shi.
Hoist your sail when the wind is fair.
Seize the opportunity.

289 Ning zuo ji tou, bu zuo niu hou.
Better to be the head of a chicken than the tail
of a cow.

290 Xin ji chi bu de re zhou.
The impatient should not try to eat scalding
hot gruel.

291 Yi nian zhi ji zai yu chun,
yi ri zhi ji zai yu chen.
The whole year's work depends on a good plan
in the spring; the whole day's work depends
on a good start in the morning.

Jia 292 Bu dang jia, bu zhi cai mi gui;
bu sheng zi, bu zhi fu mu en.
You don't know the price of fuel and rice
until you've run a household; you don't know
the love of a parent until you've had children
of your own.

293 Dang jia cai zhi cai mi gui,
chu men cai xiao lu nan xing.
Run a household and you'll know the cost of
fuel and rice; take a trip and you'll realize the
difficulty of the journey.

294 Jia bu he, wai ren qi.
Disharmony within the home leads to attacks
from without.

295 Jia jia you ben nan nian de jing.
Every household has its own tale of woe.

296 Jia li you ge jie yue shou,
yi nian chi chuan dou bu chou.
If there is a thrifty person in the family,
you'll always have enough to eat and to wear.

297 Lin jia shi huo, bu jiu zi wei.
When the neighbor's house is on fire, you put
yourself in danger if you don't help extinguish
it.

298 Ni kan wo jia hao, wo kan ni jia hao.
The grass is greener on the other side of the
fence.

Jian

299 Cheng jian bu ke you, ding jian bu ke wu.
One should maintain firm views without
becoming prejudiced.

300 Feng nian jian, zai nian zu.
Be thrifty in good times to survive in bad
times.

301 Li jian hai yao kao qiang gong.
A sharp arrow still requires a strong bow.

302 Wu jian bu xian zhong.
Without traitors, the loyal do not stand out.

303 You jian ru she yi, you she ru jian nan.
It is easy to go from frugality to extravagance;
but hard to go from extravagance to
frugality.

Jiang

304   Bu pa lang tou gao, jiu pa jiang bu qi.
Be more concerned about the oars than the
high waves.

305   Hao jiang bu shuo dang nian yong.
The good general does not refer to his past
exploits.

306   Jiang shi lao de la.
With age comes wisdom.

307   Jing gong jiang bu ru qiao zhu ren.
Better an intelligent master than a skilled
craftsman.

308   Liang jiang wu qi cai.
The skilled craftsman will discard nothing.

309   Qiang jiang shou xia wu ruo bing.
The skilled commander will lead an army of
skilled soldiers.

310   San ge chou pi jiang,
sheng guo yi ge zhu ge lang.
The wisdom of the masses exceeds that of the
wisest individual.
Two heads are better than one.

311   Yi ge hao pi jiang, mei you hao xie yang;
er ge ben pi jiang, zuo shi hao shang liang.
Two heads are better than one.

Jiao

312   Bu shi jiao de ren bu bu dao yu.
Those who don't get their feet wet don't catch
fish.

313 Bu xi jiao, bu zhi wei.
You can't appreciate the taste if you don't chew it thoroughly.

314 Jiao qian bu ke yan shen.
With casual acquaintances, engage not in deep conversation.

315 Jun zi zhi jiao dan ru shui.
Friendship between gentlemen appears indifferent but is pure like water.

316 Qing jiao bie ren bu kui ben.
It costs nothing to ask for advice.

317 Tan duo jiao bu lan.
If you stuff your mouth full, you can't chew thoroughly.

318 Xi jiao man yan, shou huo bai nian.
Chewing carefully and swallowing slowing will make for a long life.

Jie 319 Jie yue hao bi yan xian ni,
lang fei hao bi he jue di.
Thrift is like a bird carrying a pinch of earth in its bill; extravagance is like a dam that has burst.

320 Mei feng jia jie bei si qin.
On festive occasions more than ever we think of our dear ones far away.

321 Xing chuan kao zhang duo, li jia kao jie yue.
Oarsmanship is vital to ship navigation, as thrift is vital to managing a household.

322   You jie you huan, zai jie bu nan.
Return what you have borrowed and you may
borrow again.

323   Jia you qian jin, bu ji ri jin fen wen.
Better to have a modest but steady income than
one thousand pieces of gold.

324   Jin kai kou, man xu nuo.
Be prudent in speeches and promises.

325   Jin pin huo lian, ren ping xin jiao.
Gold is forged in fire, as friendship is formed
through open hearts.

326   Jin yu man tang mo zhi neng shou.
Amass a store of gold and jade, and no one can
protect it.

327   Ning she yi kuai jin, bu she yi xun chun.
Better to give away a piece of gold than to give
away a spell of time.

328   Pian di jie huang jin, zhuan deng qin ku ren.
Everywhere there is wealth waiting to be taken
by the industrious.

329   Qian jin nan mai xin tou yuan.
One thousand pieces of gold can't buy what
you long for in your heart.

330   Shi luo cun jin rong yi zhao,
cuo guo guang yi wu chu xun.
A lost bit of gold may be found,
but not lost time.

331 Zhen jin bu pa huo lian.
Genuine gold fears no fire.

Jing 332 Hao jing bu chang zai.
Good times don't last long.

333 Ni jing ren yi cun, ren jing ni yi zhang.
Extend an inch of respect, and receive a foot
in return.

334 Ru jing sui su.
When in Rome do as the Romans do.

335 Xin jing zi ran liang.
As long as one keeps calm, one doesn't feel the
heat too much.

336 Yi dong bu ru yi jing.
Quietude is superior to activity.

337 Yi ren kai jing, qian jia yin shui.
If one person builds a well, one thousand
families will have water to drink.

Jiu 338 Jiu de bu qu, xin de bu lai.
If the old is not gone, the new will not come.

339 Jiu hou tu zhen yan.
In wine there is truth.

340 Jiu neng cheng shi, jiu neng bai shi.
Wine can make you succeed or make you fail.

341 Qing jiu hong ren mian, cai bo dong ren xin.
Clear wine reddens the face, and wealth arouses
the emotions.

Ju

342 Dang ju zhe mi, pang guan zhe qing.
Spectators see the chess game better than the
players.

343 Hao ju bu ru hao san.
Better to depart on good terms than to arrive
on good terms.

Jun

344 Chu jun zi yi, chu xiao ren jian.
It's easy to get along with a gentleman,
but not so with a scoundrel.

345 Jun zi bao chou, shi nian bu wan.
Ten years is not too long for a gentleman to
wait to get revenge.

346 Jun zi bu shi chi zi zhi xin.
The gentleman is one who has not lost the
heart of a child.

347 Jun zi you cheng ren zhi mei.
The gentleman remains ready to help others
achieve their goals.

348 Neng yan bu shi zhen jun zi,
shan chu cai shi da zhang fu.
The true gentleman is not revealed by his
eloquence, but by his good conduct.

349 Yang jun ru yang hu, hu da bi shang ren.
Training soldiers is like training tigers - when
the tiger is grown it will injure others.

350 Zhi gei jun zi kan men,
bu gei xiao ren dang jia.
Better to be the doorman for a gentleman than
the manger for a knave.

K

351   Hao de kai shi shi cheng gong de yi ban.
        Well begun is half done.

352   Kao ren dou shi jia, die dao zi ji pa.
        You can't rely on others - if you fall down,
        pick yourself up.

353   Yi ke qian jin.
        Every moment is precious.

354   Xiang ma wu hao kou, xiang da wu hao shou.
        The good mouth doesn't curse and the good
        hand doesn't fight.

355   Bu chang huang lian ku, na zhi feng mi tian.
        He who has not tasted bitter knows not sweet.

356   Chi de ku zhong ku, fang wei ren shang ren.
        Suffering makes one a better person.

357   Ku jin gan lai.
        When bitterness is gone, sweetness begins.

358   Ren sheng zui ku lao lai gu.
        Loneliness in old age is the worst bitterness in
        life.

359 Xian ku hou gan, fu gui wan nian.
Taste bitter before sweet and enjoy years of
good fortune.

Kua 360 Lao wang mai gua, zi mai zi kua.
Every cook commends his own sauce.

Kuai 361 Zhu ren wei kuai le zhi ben.
Happiness is helping others.

Kui 362 Bai ri bu zuo kui xin shi,
ban ye bu pa gui qiao men.
The person with a clear conscience is not
jumpy when someone makes a midnight knock
on the door.

363 Chi yi hui kui, xue yi hui guai.
Those who are taken advantage of become
wiser for it.

L

364   Hao lai bu ru hao qu.
Better to depart on good terms than to arrive
on good terms.

365   Lai er bu wang fei li ye.
It's impolite not to give after receiving.

366   Zhi you lan ren, mei you lan di.
There are lazy people but not lazy fields.

367   Chang jiang hou lang tui qian lang,
yi dai geng bi yi dai qiang.
As one wave pushes the next, new generations
surpass old ones.

368   Lang zi hui tou jin bu huan.
The prodigal son who reforms is more
precious than gold.

369   Bu pa ren lao, zhi pa xin lao.
Old age matters not to the young at heart.

370   Huo dao lao, xue dao lao.
One is never too old to learn.

371   Jia zhong you yi lao, hao si you yi bao.
An elder in the home is like a treasure.

372   Lao ren xiu qu shao nian qi.
Old men shouldn't marry young wives.

373   Ren lao yi xin zhong.
The elderly are the most suspicious.

374   Shi lao jiu bing.
Old age brings illness.

375   Shu lao gen duo, ren lao shi duo.
As an old tree has many roots, an old person has much knowledge.

Le   376   Le ji sheng bei.
Excessive joy leads to sorrow.

Lei   377   Lei sheng da, yu dian xiao.
Thunder roars loudly, but little rain falls.

Leng   378   Tian leng bu dong mang ren.
Cold weather doesn't chill a busy person.

Li   379   Bo li duo xiao sheng yi hao.
The lower the profit margin, the greater the volume.

380   Gong li sheng qiang quan.
Truth is more powerful than force.

381   Gong shuo gong you li, po shuo po you li.
Husband and wife both say they are right.
There are two sides to every issue.

382   Gu you zhi yi wei li, wu zhi yi wei yong.
Profit comes from what is there,
usefulness from what is not there.

383   Hun li pu zhang, liang bai ju shang.
An extravagant wedding hurts both sides of the
family.

384   Li bu bian bu ming, hua bu jiang bu qing.
Truth is established through debate, as words
become clear when spoken.

385   Li duo bi zha.
Excessive politeness conceals deceit.

386   Li run da, feng xian da.
If the profits are great, the risks are great.

387   Li zhi hao ren, fa zhi huai ren.
Good people are ruled by the rules of
propriety, while bad people are ruled by laws.

388   Ning chi hao li yi ge, bu chi lan li yi kuang.
Better to eat a single good pear than a basket of
rotten ones.

389   Yi li tong, bai li ming.
Know one truth completely and understand all
truths.

390   Yi shi qiang ruo zai yu li,
qian gu sheng bai zai yu li.
Temporary gain or loss is determined by your
strength, but long-term victory or defeat is
determined by your adherence to truth.

391   You li bu zai sheng gao.
Truth is not determined by the volume of the
voice.

392　You li zou pian tian xia,
　　　wu li cun bu nan xing.
　　　When you are in the right, you can go
　　　anywhere; when you are in the wrong,
　　　you can go nowhere.

393　You yi li bi you yi bi.
　　　Where there is a pro there is a con.

394　Zhen li yu bian yu ming.
　　　Truth emerges from vigorous debate.

Lian　　395　Yi tian bu lian shou jiao man,
　　　liang tian bu lian diu yi ban.
　　　Fail to practice once and your skills will
　　　fall behind; fail to practice twice and your
　　　skills will be gone.

Liang　396　Hui da hui suan, liang shi bu duan.
　　　He who plans well will always have food.

397　Mai wu kan liang, qu qi kan niang.
　　　When buying a house, check the beams;
　　　when choosing a wife, check her mother.

398　Shang liang bu zheng, xia liang wai.
　　　If the upper beam is not straight, the lower
　　　ones will be crooked. A fish begins to stink at
　　　the head.

399　Xian dan nan zhi mei liang xin.
　　　For one without a conscience, even the elixir
　　　of life is useless.

Liao　400　Liao sheng yu wu.
　　　A little is better than none.

Lin   401   Du mu bu cheng lin.
                        A single tree does not a forest make.

               402   Jin lin bu ke duan, yuan you bu ke shu.
                        Get along with your neighbors and keep in
                        contact with distant friends.

Ling   403   Jie ling hai xu xi ling ren.
                        The one who creates the mess should
                        untangle it.

Long   404   Kun long ye you shang tian shi.
                        Even troubled dragons will get a chance to fly.
                        Every dog has his day.

               405   Long sheng long, feng sheng feng,
                        hao zi sheng lai hui da dong.
                        A dragon will produce a dragon, a phoenix
                        will produce a phoenix, and the baby mouse
                        already knows how to dig a hole.
                        Like father, like son.

               406   Long you qian shui zao xia xi,
                        hu luo ping yang bei quan qi.
                        When the dragon dives in shallow water,
                        he'll be jeered by the shrimp; when the tiger
                        descends to the valley, he be picked on by
                        the dog.

               407   Qin long yao xia hai, da hu yao shang shan.
                        You must go to sea to catch a dragon, and you
                        must climb a mountain to catch a tiger.

               408   Yao chi long rou, zi ji xia hai.
                        If you want to eat dragon meat, you'll have to
                        go out and get it yourself.

Lou

409   Bu lou chen tian qing, du shu chen nian qing.
Repair the roof while the sky is clear; acquire knowledge while you are still young.

410   Wan zhang gao lou ping di qi.
Tall buildings rise up from the ground.

Lu

411   Bu pa lu chang, zhi pa zhi duan.
A long journey will not deter one with high aspirations.

412   Chang wen lu bu mi.
You won't get lost if you frequently ask for directions.

413   Da lu you qian tiao, zhen li zhi yi tiao.
There are one thousand paths, but only one true path.

414   Lu shi zou shou de, shi shi zou shun de.
Walk a road and it becomes familiar; do a job and it becomes easy.

415   Lu yao zhi ma li, ri jiu jian ren xin.
As a long road tests a horse's strength, time will reveal a man's character.

416   Ren wu yuan lu, bi you jin you.
If a man makes no provisions for the distant future, he will certainly encounter difficulties in the near future.

417   Ren xing qian li lu, sheng du shi nian shu.
One benefits more from taking a trip than from reading about it.

418   Shi bu jing bu dong, lu bu zou bu ping.
      You can't understand what you have not
      undergone, as the road not traveled will not be
      smooth.

419   Tian wu jue ren zhi lu.
      There is always a way out.

420   Yi ren xiu lu, wan ren an bu.
      One man builds a road, and ten thousand men
      can safely travel upon it.

421   Zou jin qi qu lu, zi you ping tan tu.
      After a rough road comes a smooth path.

M

Ma

422 Bie zi zhao ma fan.
Let sleeping dogs lie.

423 Chang ma bu jing, chang da bu ling.
Excessive scoldings and beatings lose their
intended effect.

424 Hao ma bu chi hui tou cao.
A good horse will not turn back for a
mouthful of grass.

425 Hao ma bu ting ti, hao niu bu ting li.
A good horse never stops moving and a good
ox never stops pulling.

426 Lao ma shi tu.
The old horse knows the way.

427 Ma hao bu zai chao, ren mei bu zai mao.
The worth of a horse is not judged by the noise
it makes, and a person's beauty is not judged
by the external appearance.

428 Ma kao an zhuang, ren kao yi zhuang.
Fine feathers make fine birds.

429 Ma lao shi lu tu, ren lao tong shi gu.
An old horse knows the road, and an old
person knows the ways of the world.

430 Ma que sui xiao, wu zang ju quan.
A sparrow may be small but it has everything
it needs.

431 Ma yi ban jia, da yu jiang xia.
When ants look for a new home, it portends a
heavy rain.

432 You yao ma er pao de kuai,
you yao ma er bu chi cao.
You can't expect the horse to run fast
if you don't let it graze.

433 Yuan zi li pao bu chu qian li ma.
A strong steed cannot be raised in the yard.

Mai 434 Mai jin tian xia wu, nan mai zi sun xian.
You can buy anything for a price except virtue
for your offspring.

Man 435 Man bu die bu dao, xiao xin cuo bu liao.
Walk slowly and you won't fall down; act
carefully and you won't make mistakes.

436 Man zhao sun, qian shou yi.
One loses by pride and gains by modesty.

Mao 437 Hao jiao de mao dai bu zhu lao shu.
Cats that love to purr don't catch mice.

438 Lan mao dai bu zhu si lao shu.
The lazy cat won't even catch a dead mouse.

439 Mao fa wei ye cheng bu liao lao hu.
The cat may shriek, but it will never become a tiger.

440 Mei mao shi quan neng, jin qian shi wan neng.
Beauty is potent but money is omnipotent.

441 Na ge mao er bu chi lao shu.
Show me a cat that won't eat a mouse.

442 Ren bu ke mao xiang.
You can't judge a person on his appearance.

443 Wai mao rong yi ren, nei xin zui nan cai.
It's easy to recognize appearances, but difficult to fathom the mind.

444 Zui shang wu mao, ban shi bu lao.
Youth have no experience and can't be trusted with important jobs.

Mei 445 Shi ge mei po jiu ge huang.
Nine out of ten matchmakers are liars.

Men 446 Chu men kan tian se, mai mai kan hang qing.
When you leave the house, check the weather; when you do business, check the market.

447 Hao men duo nie zi.
Rich families have more sinners.

Meng 448 Meng sui xin sheng.
Our dreams reflect our mind.

Mi 449 Bai mi ye you yi shu.
You can't cover every base.

450 Sheng mi zhu cheng shu fan.
When rice is cooked, it's cooked.
What is done is done.

451 Yi yang mi yang bai yang ren.
One kind of rice will nourish one hundred
kinds of people.

Mian 452 Bu shi lu shan zhen mian mu, zhi yuan shen
zai ci shan zhong.
When I am standing on Mt. Lu, I see not the
true face of Mt. Lu.

Miao 453 Dao shen me miao, shao shen me xiang.
Burn the right incense in the right temple.
When in Rome, do as the Romans.

Min 454 Min yi shi wei tian.
To the common folk, food is heaven.

Ming 455 Bu pa sheng huai ming, jiu pa sheng huai bing.
Be more concerned about a bad illness than
about bad fate.

456 Jian ting ze ming, pian xin ze an.
Listen to both sides and be enlightened;
listen to one side and be deceived.

457 Mei ming nan de er yi shi.
A good reputation is hard to earn but easy to
lose.

458 Ming ke ming fei chang ming.
The name that can be named is not the eternal
name.

459 Ming li er zi shi fei duo.
Fame and fortune lead to much trouble.

460 Ming ren bu zuo an shi.
The honest person doesn't do shady things.

461 Ming zhao an shi, li fu ren xin.
As light brightens a dark room, truth wins
man's heart.

462 Ren guo liu ming, yan guo liu sheng.
A person leaves behind his name, as a goose
leaves behind its call.

463 Ren pa chu ming, zhu pa zhuang.
As fattening portends trouble for pigs, fame
portends trouble for a man.

Mou 464 Jiang zai mou er bu zai yong,
bing zai jing er bu zai duo.
Generals are valued for their strategic abilities
rather than their battlefield courage;
soldiers are valued for their quality rather than
their quantity.

Mu 465 Du mu bu cheng lin.
A single tree does not a forest make.

466 Gang mu yi zhe, qiang gong yi duan.
Hard wood and strong bows break easily.

467 Yan shuang jian zhen mu.
The best wood is found in harsh climates.

N

Nai	468	You nai bian shi niang. She who provides milk is regarded as mother.
Nan	469	Huan nan jian zhen qing. A friend in need is a friend indeed.
	470	Tian xia wu nan shi, zhi pa you xin ren. Where there is a will, there is a way.
Neng	471	Neng zhe duo lao. The capable are assigned more tasks.
Niang	472	Qin niang dai chu lan er zi. The mother who provides everything will raise a lazy son.
Niao	473	Niao zhi jiang si, qi ming ye ai; ren zhi jiang si, qi yan ye shan. When a bird is about to die, it cries plaintively; when a man is about to die, he speaks benevolently.
	474	Ning wei wu shang niao, bu zuo fang li qie. Better to be a free bird on the roof than a wealthy concubine in the house.
	475	Yi niao zai shou, sheng guo bai niao zai lin. A bird in the hand is better than two in the bush.

Niu

476   Lao niu hao shi.
Old cows are obedient.

477   Niu da ya bu liao shi zi.
A large bull cannot pick his own lice.

Nu

478   Huan chang nu er zhen wu qing.
Women who enjoy the nightlife have the
hardest hearts.

479   Ning fan tian gong nu, mo fan zhong ren nao.
Better to anger heaven than to anger the
masses.

480   Nu da shi ba bian.
When girls grow up, they undergo many
changes.

481   Nu da shi ba yi zhi hua.
A girl of eighteen is like a flower.

482   Ren yi shi zhi nu, ke mian bai ri zhi you.
Restrain yourself in a moment of anger, and
you'll avoid long periods of sorrow.

483   Sheng nu zhi xia shi shi wei ren.
True character is revealed in moments of
extreme anger.

484   Xiao ren wu, yi fa nu.
The little pot is soonest hot.

485   Zhong nu nan fan.
It's dangerous to incur the wrath of the masses.

P

Pa   486   Pa de gao, die de zhong.
The higher you climb, the harder you fall.

Pang   487   Yi kou chi bu cheng ge pang zi.
Obesity is not the result of a single bite.

Peng   488   Jiu rou peng you hao zhao,
huan nan zhi jiao nan feng.
It's easy to find friends for a party, it's hard to
find friends in time of trouble.

Pi   489   Pi ji tai lai.
Calm follows a storm.

490   Pi zhi bu cun, mao jiang yan fu.
When the skin is gone, to what can the hair
adhere?
Everything needs its foundation.

Ping   491   Kou shuo wu ping, shi shi wei zheng.
The proof of the pudding is in the eating.

492   Man ping bu xiang, ban ping huang dang.
A full bottle makes no sound, a half full bottle
sloshes around.

493   Ren ping bu yu, shui ping bu liu.
Justice leads to peace.

Po

494   Jiu zhu po, bu xian dou.
Those who live long on the hillside do not mind the slope.

495   Po you de, xi fu xian.
Virtuous mother-in-law, virtuous daughter-in-law.

Q

496   Jia you xian qi, fu you xian yi.
Good wife, carefree life.

497   Qi da shang shen, shi duo shang shen.
Excessive anger harms the spirit, excessive food
harms the body.

498   Qi gai wu zhong, lan han zi cheng.
One becomes a lazy beggar through no fault
but his own

499   Qi ke gu er bu ke xie.
Morale should be boosted, not dampened.

500   Qi xiao yi ying.
Small vessels are easy to fill.

501   Qi zhe bu li.
He who stands on tiptoe is not steady.

502   Qu qi qiu shu nu.
For a wife, seek a lady.

503   Qu qi qu de, bu qu se.
Marry a woman for her virtue, not for her looks.

504   Ren zheng qi, huo zheng yan.
People strive for high spirits as fire strives to become flames.

505   Zheng qi gao, xie qi xiao.
A healthy atmosphere drives away evil.

Qian   506   Bei qian suo fei zhe, wei bi jie dao qie.
Not everyone that a dog barks at is a thief.

507   Chi yi qian, zhang yi zhi.
A fall in the pit, a gain in your wit.

508   Dao chu bu yong qian, chu chu re ren xian.
If you don't spend your money, you won't be welcome anywhere.

509   Jiu peng fan you, mei qian fen shou.
Friends made during merrymaking scatter when the money runs out.

510   Qian cai shen wai wu.
Money is not inherent to man.

511   Qian cai yue hua yue shao,
zhi shi yue xue yue duo.
The more you spend, the less you have;
the more you study, the more you know.

512   Qian dao gong shi ban, huo dao zhu tou lan.
Money greases the wheel for a business, as fire roasts a succulent pig.

513 Qian dao guang gun shou, yi qu bu hui tou.
Money, in the hands of a bachelor, is as good as gone.

514 Qian neng tong shen.
Money allows you to speak to the gods.

515 Qian ren zhong shu, hou ren cheng liang.
Each generation will reap what the former generation has sown.

516 Qian shi bu wang, hou shi zhi shi.
The past remembered is a good guide for the future.

517 Qian xu shi cheng gong de peng you.
Modesty is the companion of success.

518 Ren zhuan qian nan, qian zhuan qian rong yi.
Easy for money to make money, hard for man to make money.

519 Wu qian bu cheng shi.
Everything requires money to succeed.

520 Xia zi jian qian yan jing kai.
Even a blind man opens his eyes when he encounters money.

521 Yi fen qian, yi fen huo.
You get what you pay for.

522 Yi qian fei xing, bai qian fei sheng.
One dog barks at a shape, and one hundred dogs bark at the sound.

523 Yong ren qian cai, ti ren xiao zai.
If you take someone's money, you must help him take care of his business.

524 You qian ban shi chen xin yi.
Money helps you get your way.

525 You qian chang xiang wu qian ri,
feng nian chang ji da huang nian.
Think of days of poverty when you have money, and remember the lean years when reaping a rich harvest.

526 You qian gai bai chou.
Money conceals ugliness.

527 You qian nan mai hou hui yao.
No amount of money will buy medicine for regrets.

528 You qian nan mai shao nian shi.
Money cannot buy back your youth.

529 You qian neng shi gui tui mo.
With money you can make the ghost work the mill. Money can work miracles.

530 You qian yi tiao long, wu qian yi tiao chong.
With money, you are a dragon;
lacking money, you are a bug.

Qiang 531 Chai dong qiang, bu xi qiang,
jie guo hai shi zhu po fang.
If you tear down the right wall to fix the left wall, you'll still have a broken wall.

532 Ge qiang you er.
Walls have ears.

533 Ming qiang yi duo, an jian nan fang.
It is easy to dodge a spear in the open, but hard
to guard against an arrow shot from hiding.

534 Ni qiang kun nan ruo, ni ruo kun nan qiang.
If your mind is strong, all difficult things will
become easy; if your mind is weak, all easy
things will become difficult.

535 Qi qiang xian da ji, chi dan xian yang ji.
You must lay a foundation before you build a
wall, and you must raise a chicken before you
gather eggs.
Sow and you shall reap.

536 Qiang dao zhong ren tui.
When a wall is about to collapse, everybody
gives it a push.
Everybody hits a man who is down.

537 Qiang you feng, bi you er.
Walls have ears.

538 Qiang zhong zi you qiang zhong shou.
However strong you are, there is always
someone stronger.

539 Yi jia qi qiang, liang jia hao kan.
When one family builds a wall, two families
enjoy it.

Qiao 540 Qiao zhe duo lao jue zhe xian.
The clever are entrusted with many tasks while
the dull remain idle.

Qin

541 Qin lao yi shou, an yi wang shen.
Industry leads to longevity; leisure leads to
doom.

542 Qin shi yao qian shu, jian shi ju bao pen.
Diligence is the tool that brings one riches and
frugality is the measure that helps keep them.

543 Qin wei wu jia bao, shen shi hu shen fu.
Diligence is a priceless treasure, and caution is a
talisman for survival.

544 Qin yi bu zhuo.
Diligence will compensate for lack of natural
skill.

545 Qin yi zhi fu.
Diligence leads to riches.

546 Qin you gong, xi wu yi.
Achievement comes from diligence, and
nothing is gained by fooling around.

547 Ren qin di sheng bao, ren lan di sheng cao.
The diligent grow treasures in the field, but the
lazy grow weeds.

548 Shu shan you lu qin wei jing.
Diligence is the royal road to learning.

549 Yi qin sheng bai qiao, yi lan sheng bai bing.
Diligence produces much ingenuity while
laziness creates many illnesses.

550 Yuan qin bu ru jin lin.
Neighbors are dearer than distant relatives.

551 Zhi qin mei jian, you zhen mei xian.
Diligence without frugality is like a needle
without thread.

Qing 552 Qing hai wu feng, bo lang zi qi.
Love itself is calm; the turbulence arrives from
individuals.

553 Qing ren yan li chu xi shi.
Beauty is in the eye of the beholder.

554 Shui huo wu qing.
Floods and fires have no mercy.

Qiong 555 Qiong bu ke qi, fu bu ke chi.
Do not take advantage of the poor; do not rely
on the rich.

556 Qiong ze bian, bian ze tong.
Impasse is followed by change, and change will
lead to a solution.

557 Qiong ze du shan qi shen,
da ze jian shan tian xia.
When poor, you take care of yourself;
when well-off, you take care of everyone.

558 Shi bu qiong, chuan bu qiong,
bu hui da suan yi shi qiong.
You can't eat or clothe yourself into the
poorhouse; only when you can't manage your
affairs will you be forever poor.

559 Yu qiong qian li mu, geng shang yi ceng lou.
If you want to see farther, you have to go
higher.

Qiu 560 Ren bu qiu ren yi ban da.
When no one begs, all are equal.

561 Ren dao wu qiu pin zi gao.
One with no desires has an exalted character.

Qu 562 Qu gao he gua.
With high-brow songs, very few people will
join in the chorus.

Quan 563 Da ren yi quan, fang ren yi jiao.
If you strike someone with your fist, beware of
a kick in return.

Que 564 Bai yang que er bai yang yin.
One hundred different sparrows make one
hundred different sounds.

R

565 De rao ren chu qie rao ren.
Pardon others when you can.

566 Re ji sheng feng.
Extreme heat produces wind.

567 Ji suo bu yu, wu shi yu ren.
Do not do to others what you would not like
others to do to you.

568 Mou shi zai ren, cheng shi zai tian.
Man proposes, God disposes.

569 Qiu ren bu ru qiu ji.
Better to help yourself than ask for help from
others.

570 Ren bu zai da xiao, ma bu zai gao di.
Men are not judged by their size, and horses
are not judged by their height.

571 Ren bu zhi ji chou, ma bu zhi lian chang.
Man sees not his own ugliness, and horses are
unaware of the length of their heads.

572 Ren ding sheng tian.
Man will triumph over nature.

573 Ren duo zui za.
Agreement is difficult if there are too many people.

574 Ren fei cao mu, shu neng wu qing.
Men are not plants, they all have feelings.

575 Ren fei shen xian, shu neng wu guo?
Men are not saints, how can they be free from faults?

576 Ren ge you suo hao.
Every man has his preference.

577 Ren hui bian, yue hui yuan.
People change, as the moon waxes.

578 Ren qin di bu lan.
Where the tiller is tireless, the land is fertile.

579 Ren wang gao chu pa, shui wang di chu liu.
People seek high places, and water seeks low places.

580 Ren wu lian chi, bai shi ke wei.
If a man is impervious to shame, he can do all sorts of evil.

581 Ren zai shi shang lian, dao zai shi shang mo.
The world refines a man, as a stone sharpens a knife.

582 Ren zhe jian ren, zhi zhe jian zhi.
The benevolent see benevolence, and the wise see wisdom. Different people have different points of view.

583 Ren zi jia zhong bao.
Tolerance is the treasure of the home.

584 Sheng lao bing shi, ren zhi chang qing.
Birth, aging, sickness, and death - such is the lot of every man.

585 Tian bu sheng wu yong zhi ren,
di bu zhang wu ming zhi cao.
There are no useless people, as there are no plants without a name.

586 Tui ji ji ren.
Do unto others as you would have them do unto you.

Ri 587 Ri guang bu zhao men, yi sheng jiu shang men.
The home where sunlight never enters will be visited often by the doctor.

588 Wu shi xian ri chang, you shi xian ri duan.
Time flies when you are having fun.

Rou 589 Rou neng ke gang.
Gentleness overcomes harshness.

Ruan 590 Qi ruan bi pa ying.
Those who bully the weak are cowards before the strong.

S

San 591 Tian xian wu bu san de yan xi.
All good things come to an end.

Se 592 Bu se bu liu, bu zhi bu xing.
There is no flowing without stoppage, and no
motion without rest.

593 Mei se wu mei de, hao bi hua wu xiang.
Beauty without virtue is like a flower with no
fragrance.

Sha 594 Ju sha cheng ta.
Many grains of sand piled up will make a
pagoda.
Many a little makes a mickle.

595 Kuai zhi wu hao sha, kuai jia wu hao jia.
Weave fast and the yarn is no good;
marry in haste and the family is no good.

596 Sha li sui xiao shang ren yan.
Sand is minute, but it will harm your eyes.

Shan 597 Bu shang gao shan, bu xian ping di.
If you don't climb a high mountain, you
won't see the valley.

598 Cong shan ru deng, cong e ru beng.
Pursuit of the good is like climbing;
pursuit of evil is like collapsing.

599 Ji shan zhe chang.
Those who accumulate good deeds will
prosper.

600 Ji shan zhi jia, bi you yu qing.
Those who accumulate good deeds will have
many to celebrate.

601 Jiang shan yi gai, ben xing nan yi.
Rivers can be channeled and mountain moved;
the hardest thing is to change the ways of man.
The leopard cannot change his spots.

602 Kao shan chi shan, kao shui chi shui.
Those living on the mountain live off of the
mountain; those living near water, live off of
the water. Make use of local resources.

603 Lai zhe bu shan, shan zhe bu lai.
He who has come is surely strong, or he'd
never have come along.

604 Liu de qing shan zai, bu pa mei cai shao.
As long as there are forests, one need not
worry about firewood.

605 Ren jian dao chu you qing shan.
Forests exist everywhere in the world.
The sun shines upon all alike.

606   Ren shan bei ren qi, ma shan bei ren qi.
The good person will be taken advantage of by
others, as the tame horse will be ridden.

607   Shan bu ji, bu zu yi cheng min.
If you don't do good deeds, you will not build
a good reputation.

608   Shan shi shan zhong.
Start well and end well.

609   Shan shi ze gong jin yu cheng.
Well begun is half done.

610   Shang shan ruo shui.
The highest good is like water.

611   Wei shan chang le.
The pleasure of doing good is the only one that
will not wear out.

612   Xue shan san nian, xue e yi zhao.
It takes three years to learn something good,
but a day to learn something bad.

613   Yao zhi shan zhong shi, xu wen da cai ren.
If you want to know what is happening in the
mountain, you must ask the wood collector.

614   Yi shan nan rong er hu.
One mountain can't host two tigers.
When Greek meets Greek, a tug of war ensues.

615   You shan bi you lu, you shui bi you du.
Where there is a mountain, there is a pass;
where there is water, there is a ferry.
Nature provides a remedy.

Shang

616 Zhe shan wang zhe na shan gao.
The grass is always greener on the other side of the fence.

Shang

617 Dao shang yi zhi, kou shang nan yi.
Easy to cure the cut of a knife,
difficult to cure the cut of words.
Words cut more than swords.

Shao

618 Ji shao cheng duo.
Many a little makes a mickle.

619 Shao nian bu zhi qin xue zao,
bai tou fang hui du shu chi.
Study hard when you are young,
or you'll regret it when you are old.

620 Shao zhuang bu nu li, lao da tu shang bei.
Laziness in youth spells regret in old age.

She

621 Ren xin bu zu she tun xiang.
Greedy people are like snakes trying to swallow an elephant.

622 She chang shi zhang, ye chang meng duo.
With a long tongue, affairs will multiply;
in a long night, dreams will multiply.

623 She jian li yu dao jian.
The tongue cuts deeper than the sword.

624 Yi zhao bei she yao, shi nian pa cao sheng.
Once bitten by a snake, one shies away from a coiled rope for the next ten years.
Once bitten, twice shy.

Shen 625 Bu hui shao xiang de zui shen,
bu hui jiang hua de zui ren.
If you know not how to pray, you offend the
gods; if you know not how to talk, you offend
others.

626 Jian quan zhi jing shen,
yu yu jian quan zhi shen ti.
Sound mind in sound body.

627 Ning ke shen leng, bu ke xin leng.
Better a cold body than a cold heart.

628 Qiu shen bu ru qiu ren.
Better to ask a favor from others than from
a god.

629 Shen jiao sheng yu yan jiao.
Example is better than precept.

Sheng 630 Hou sheng ke wei.
The younger generation will surpass the
older.
Every oak was once an acorn.

631 Jiu du wu sheng jia.
There are no winners among habitual
gamblers.

632 Ren fei sheng er zhi zhi, nai xue er zhi zhi.
At birth we know nothing, knowledge
comes from learning.

633 Ren sheng qi shi cai kai shi.
Life begins at seventy.

634   Ren zhi sheng ye ruo ruo, qi si ye jian qiang.
We are born gentle and weak, but are hard and stiff at death.

635   San tian bu nian kou sheng,
san nian bu zuo shou sheng.
Fall behind in practice and your skills will fade.

636   Sheng bai nai bing jia chang shi.
For a military commander, victory or defeat is a common occurrence.

637   Sheng bu jiao, bai bu nie.
Become not dizzy with success, nor disheartened by failure.

638   Sheng en bu ru yang en.
Birth is much, but breeding is more.

639   Sheng you ya er zhi wu ya.
Life is limited, but knowledge is unlimited.

640   Sheng yu you huan, si yu an le.
Life springs from sorrow and calamity;
death results from ease and pleasure.

641   Yi hui sheng, er hui shou.
First time strangers, second time friends.
First time awkward, second time skilled.

642   Yi ri sheng yi ba, san nian mai pi ma.
Save a little every day, and you can buy a horse in three years.
Many drops make a shower.

643 Bu jing yi shi, bu zhang yi zhi.
You can't gain knowledge without practice.
Wisdom comes from experience.

644 Bu pa shi qing nan, jiu pa bu nai fan.
No task is too difficult if you are patient.

645 Guan xian shi, luo bu shi.
Mind other's business and you will get blamed
in the end.

646 Gun shi bu sheng tai, zhuan ye bu ju cai.
A rolling stone gathers no moss.

647 Hao shi bu chu men, huai shi chuan qian li.
Good news travels slowly, bad news travels
fast.

648 Hao shi mo dao ye yao shui.
When sharpening a knife, even the finest stone
needs water.

649 Jin ri shi, jin ri bi.
Today's work, today's finish.

650 Shi bai shi cheng gong zhi mu.
Failure is the mother of success.

651 Shi bi shou gen you fu.
It's better to give than to receive.

652 Shi cheng yu he mu, li sheng yu tuan jie.
Undertakings succeed from harmony,
and strength results from unity.

653 Shi fei jing guo bu zhi nan.
One does not realize the difficulty of an
undertaking unless he has experienced it
before.

654 Shi fei nan tao zhong kou.
Public opinion is the arbiter of right and
wrong.

655 Shi fei zhong ri you, bu ting zi ran wu.
Gossip may abound, but if you don't listen to
it, there will be no gossip.

656 Shi fei zi you gong lun.
The masses decide what is right and wrong.

657 Shi ke sha bu ke ru.
The brave man prefers death to dishonor.

658 Shi shi sheng yu xiong bian.
Facts speak louder than words.

659 Shi shi wu zhe wei jun jie.
He who comprehends the times is great.

660 Shi shi zao ying xiong.
Every age will produce its own heroes.

661 Shi sui xiao, bu zuo bu cheng;
zi sui xian, bu jiao bu ming.
Even the simplest undertaking requires effort
before it can be completed; even the ablest
child must receive instruction to become
intelligent.

662   Ta shan zhi shi, ke yi gong cuo.
       A good quality of another may provide the
       remedy for our faults.

663   Tian xia shi qi neng jin ren yi.
       Roses too have thorns.

664   Yan shi chu gao tu.
       A strict master produces a skilled apprentice.

665   Yi jia you shi, si lin bu an.
       Problems in one family produce grief for the
       whole neighborhood.

666   Yi shi fu ren kou, yi li fu ren xin.
       Force may lead to agreement but truth will
       lead to conviction.

667   You qian ren pa shi.
       The rich fear trouble.

668   Yu yuan shi fei, shen jiao wei xian.
       Choose your friends carefully if you want to
       stay out of trouble.

669   Zhi yao ku gan, shi cheng yi ban.
       Work hard and the job is half done.

670   Zuo shi rong yi, zuo ren nan.
       It's easy to do a job but difficult to conduct
       oneself properly.

671   Feng shou mei you qiao, duo chu ji bian cao.
       There's no trick to a bountiful harvest - simply
       work your hoe with diligence.

672 Hao shou nan xiu mei xian hua.
Even a skilled craftsman needs thread to
embroider a flower.

673 Liang ren yang ma shou,
liang ren yang chuan lou.
A horse raised by two people will be skinny,
and the boat taken care of by two people will
leak.

674 Qi shou ba jiao bi bai shi.
Too many cooks spoil the soup.

675 Qiao shou nan shi liang gen zhen.
Even a skilled hand cannot sew with two
needles at the same time.

676 Qin kuai ren yong shou,
lan duo ren yong kou.
Diligent persons use their hands while lazy
persons use their mouths.

677 Yi fen geng yun, yi fen shou huo.
The more ploughing and weeding the better
the harvest.

Shu 678 Da shu ye you ku zhi.
Even large trees have dry branches.

679 Hao shu bu yan bai hui du.
Good books retain their flavor after one
hundred readings.

680 Mei you wu tong shu, na zhao feng huang lai.
You cannot attract a phoenix without a paraso
tree. You cannot catch a fish without a worm.

681   Pin zhe yin shu er fu, fu zhe yin shu er gui.
        The poor are enriched by books, while the rich
        are distinguished by books.

682   Shi nian shu mu, bai nian shu ren.
        It takes ten years to grow a tree, and one
        hundred years for a sound educational program
        to take root.

683   Shu da zhao feng.
        A tall tree catches the wind. Persons in high
        places are more likely to be attacked.

684   Shu dao yong shi fang hen shao.
        When the time comes to apply knowledge, we
        regret our lack thereof.

685   Shu du bai bian, qi yi zi ming.
        Read a book one hundred times and its
        meaning will become clear.

686   Shu gao qian zhang, ye luo gui gen.
        A tree may grow tall but its leaves still
        fall back down to the roots.

687   Shu lao ban xin kong, ren lao bai shi tong.
        Old trees are hollow, but old men have
        knowledge.

688   Shu neng sheng qiao.
        Practice makes perfect.

689   Shu pa bo pi, ren pa shang xin.
        People fear a broken heart as a tree fears
        peeling bark.

690 Shu xiao fu zhi yi, shu da fu zhi nan.
You can easily straighten out a small tree;
not so a large tree.

691 Wu qiao bu cheng shu.
There is no story without coincidence.

Shui 692 Di shui chuan shi.
Constant dripping wears away the stone.

693 Fei shui bu luo wai ren tian.
Every man diverts water to his own field.

694 Fu shui nan shou.
There is no use crying over spilled milk.

695 Jing shui bu fan he shui.
Well water does not encroach upon river
water. I'll mind my business, and you mind
yours.

696 Liu shui bu fu, hu shu bu du.
Running water does not stink and a door hinge
does not become worm eaten.

697 Pa shui dang bu liao yu fu.
Those afraid of the water will never become
fishermen.

698 Shui bu liu hui chou, miao bu guan mei shou.
Stagnant water stinks, and the untended
seedling produces no crop.

799 Shui qian bu rong da zhou.
Shallow water will not support a large boat.

700 Shui shen bu xiang, xiang shui bu shen.
Deep water is silent and noisy water is not
deep.

701 Shui shen liu qu man, zhi ren hua yu chi.
Deep water flows slowly, and wise men
measure their words.

702 Shui sui ping, yi you bo;
heng sui zhun, yi you cha.
Calm water also produces waves; the calibrated
scale will also be slightly off.

703 Shui zhi qing ze wu yu.
You won't find fish in clear water.

704 Yuan shui jiu bu liao jin huo.
Distant water won't put out a fire close at
hand. An unavailable remedy is useless.

705 Yuan shui zhi bu liao jin ke.
Distant water won't quench immediate thirst.

706 Zao shui zao qi jing shen hao.
Early to bed and early to rise makes a man full
of vitality.

Shuo   707 Hao ren shuo bu huai, hao jiu jiao bu suan.
Gossip won't harm a good person as stirring
won't spoil good wine.

708 Lu shang shuo hua, cao li you ren.
Be careful about what you say - you don't
know who is listening.

709 Shuo cao cao, cao cao jiu dao.
Speak of the devil and the devil appears.

Si   710   Ning yuan jie shen er si,
                  bu yuan wu shen er sheng.
                  Death before dishonor.

            711   San si er hou xing.
                  Look before you leap.

            712   Si zhong you guo, mang zhong you cuo.
                  Selfishness and haste produce mistakes.

Su   713   Yu su ze bu da.
                  Haste makes waste.

Sui   714   Jia ji sui ji, jia gou sui gou.
                  Follow the man you marry, be he a fool or a
                  crook.

            715   Sui yue bu rao ren.
                  Time waits for no one.

            716   Sui yue tian ren shou, bei chou cui ren lao.
                  Time adds to your longevity; sorrow adds to
                  your old age.

Suo   717   Ri yue ru suo.
                  The sun and the moon move back and forth
                  like a shuttle.

T

Tai   718   Jiu ceng zhi tai qi yu lei tu.
              A nine-story terrace rises through a gradual
              accumulation of bricks and mud.

Tan   719   Tan zhe bi shi.
              Grasp all, lose all.

Tian   720   Huang tian bu fu ku xin ren.
              Heaven will reward the diligent.

       721   Man tian man di, man bu guo lin ju.
              You may deceive heaven and earth, but you
              can't deceive your neighbor.

       722   Tian bu yan zi gao, di bu yan zi hou.
              Heaven does not refer to its height, and the
              earth does not refer to its breadth.

       723   Tian cai zai yu qin fen.
              Genius comes from diligence.

       724   Tian you bu ce feng yun,
              ren you dan xi hou fu.
              In nature there are unexpected storms; in life
              there are unexpected outcomes.

725   Tian you han shu yin qing,
        ren you bei huan li he.
        In nature, there is cold, hot, cloudy, and clear;
        in life, there is sorrow, joy, separation, and
        unity.

726   Tian you hao sheng zhi de.
        Heaven provides a means for everything.

727   Tian zhu zi zhu zhe.
        Heaven helps those who help themselves.

728   Yi zhao tian zi, yi zhao chen.
        Every new sovereign brings his own courtiers.

729   You shang bu qu de tian,
        mei you guo bu qu de guan.
        There may be heights than can't be scaled, but
        there are no barriers than can't be broken.

Tiao   730   Yi ren nan tiao bai wei geng.
        You can't please all of the people all of the
        time.

731   Zhong kou nan tiao.
        You can't please all of the people all of the
        time.

Tie   732   Da tie xian dei ben shen ying.
        It takes a tough man to forge iron.

733   Da tie yao chen re.
        Strike while the iron is hot.

734 Hao tie bu da ding, hao nan bu dang bing.
Good iron is not turned into nails; good men
are not turned into soldiers.

735 Leng tie nan da, lao zhu nan wan.
Cold iron is hard to forge, and old bamboo is
hard to bend.

Ting 736 Hui shuo bu ru hui ting.
It's better to know how to listen than how to
talk.

Tong 737 Kong tong xiang ding dang.
Empty vessels make the most sound.

738 Shi shi ban tong, bu ru yi yi jing tong.
Better a master of one field than a dilettante in
ten.

739 Tong sheng xiang ying, tong qi xiang qiu.
Like attracts like.

Tou 740 Wei ren bu dang tou, wei mu bu dang zhou.
Keep out of the spotlight.

Tu 741 Jiao tu you san ku.
A clever hare has three burrows.

742 Shan e bu tong tu.
Good and evil follow different paths.

743 Wan wu sheng yu tu, wan wu gui yu tu.
Ashes to ashes, dust to dust.

744   Yi zhu er tu, yi tu bu de.
If you chase after two rabbits, you'll catch neither.

Tuan   745   Tuan jie jiu shi li liang.
Unity is strength.

746   Tuan jie li liang da, cai duo huo yan gao.
In unity there is strength, just as many pieces of wood create a large fire.

747   Tuan jie yi tiao xin, huang tu bian huang jin.
Unity can turn dirt into gold.

W

Wai | 748 | Guan qi wai er zhi qi nei.
Look at the outside and know the inside.

749 | Ren wai you ren, shan wai you shan.
However strong you are, there is always
someone stronger.

Wan | 750 | Duan ren jia wan, fu ren jia guan.
Accept from another - abandon your freedom.

751 | Wan shi qi tou nan.
Everything is hard in the beginning

752 | Yi zhi wan bu xiang, liang zhi wan ding dang.
A single bowl makes no sound, but two bowls
together will ring. It takes two to tango.

Wang | 753 | Tian wang hui hui, shu er bu lou.
God's mill grinds slowly but surely.

Wei | 754 | Shen qi wei ren, guan qi zhu you.
If you want to know someone's character, look
at the friends he keeps.

Wen | 755 | Bai wen bu ru yi jian.
Better to see once than hear one hundred times.

756   Bu zhi jiu wen, bu neng ze xue.
You should ask if you don't know, and you should study if you don't know how.

757   Er wen wei xu, yan jian wei shi.
What you hear may be false, but what you see is true.

758   Pa wen lu, yao mi lu.
Those who are afraid to ask directions will get lost.

759   Wen bian wan jia cheng hang jia.
Ask around and you'll become an expert.

760   Wen jian zha shi bi zhi sheng.
Slow and steady wins the race.

761   Wen lu bu shi li, duo zou er shi li.
If you ask for directions rudely, you may end up twenty miles from your destination.

762   Zi jia de wen zhang, ren jia de po niang.
In writing, one's own work is better; in women, the other man's is better.

Wu   763   Qiang ji bu ru shan wu.
Forced memorization is not as good as natural realization.

764   Tian xia wu ya yi ban hei.
All crows are black. Evil people are bad all over the world.

765   Wu ji bi fan.
The pendulum always swings back.

766 Wu ya bao xi mei ren xin.
No one believes a crow bearing good news.

767 Wu ya bu yu feng huang qi.
The crow doesn't perch on the same branch
as the phoenix.

768 Wu yao fang lan, ren yao fang lan.
With goods, guard against rotting;
with people, guard against laziness.

769 Wu yi lei ju.
Birds of a feather flock together.

770 Wu yi xi wei gui.
The thing which is rare is dear.

771 Yi wu xiang yi wu.
There is always one thing to subdue another.

X

772 Bei xi wei lin.
Happiness and sorrow are neighbors.

773 Qu ge xi fu fen ge jia.
Take a wife and break up a family.

774 Qu le xi fu wang le niang.
Take a wife and you will forget about your
mother.

775 Ren feng xi shi jing shen shuang.
Joy puts heart into a man.

776 Wen xi kao zui, wu xi kao tui.
Drama depends on the lips, while martial arts
depend on the legs.

777 Xi guan cheng zi ran.
Habits become second-nature.

778 Yi dai hao xi fu, san dai hao er sun.
A good wife makes for three generations of
good offspring.

Xia 779 Xian xia shou wei qiang,
hou xia shou zao yang.
Strike first and prevail; strike late and fail.

Xian 780 Dan si bu cheng xian.
A single strand of silk will not make a thread.

781 Fang chang xian, diao da yu.
Throw a long line to catch a big fish.
Adopt a long-term plan to secure something
big.

782 Ren xian sheng bing, shi xian sheng tai.
Sickness visits the idle man, as moss grows on
the embedded stone.

783 Xiao ren xian ju zuo dai shi.
Idle hands are the devil's playground.

Xiang 784 Bu pa xiang gui kong,
zhi yao you ge hao lao gong.
If you have a good husband, you need not be
concerned about an empty wardrobe.

Xiao 785 Ni yang wo xiao, wo yang ni lao.
You take care of me when I'm young,
and I take care of you when you're old.

786 Ren wu xiao lian bu kai dian.
Don't go into business without a smile.

787 Wu shi bu xiao bai bu.
The pot calls the kettle black.

788 Xiao bu ren ze luan da mou.
He who cannot endure small defeats will fail
at large tasks.

789 Xiao hai bu neng guan, yi guan ding you luan.
You can't spoil a child or it will create trouble.

790 Xiao hai zui li tu zhen yan.
Children speak the truth.

791 Xiao kou chang kai, qing chun chang zai.
Smile often and you will remain youthful.

792 Xiao men kai, xing fu lai.
A sunny disposition brings good fortune.

793 Xiao ren de cun bian jin chi.
Give knaves an inch and they will take a yard.

794 Xiao ren ji chou, jun zi gan en.
The petty man recalls minor insults while the
gentleman is filled with gratitude.

795 Xiao ren xin duo, ai shu gen duo.
Scoundrels have many tricks up their sleeves,
as short trees have many roots.

796 Xiao ren zi da, xiao xi sheng da.
Scoundrels are arrogant, just as little creeks
make the most noise.

797 Xiao shi bu zhi lao niang qin,
yu er cai zhi bao niang en.
Children don't realize how good their mother
is until they grow up and raise children of
their own.

798   Xiao shi liao liao, da wei bi jia.
       Intelligent children do not necessarily grow
       into remarkable adults.

799   Xiao shi tou zhen, da le tou jin.
       Steal a needle as a child; steal gold as an adult.

800   Xiao xin shi de wan nian chuan.
       Caution is the vehicle for a long journey.

801   Xiao xin tian xia ke zou,
       lu mang cun bu nan xing.
       Proceed with caution and
       travel everywhere; proceed recklessly and go
       nowhere.

802   Yi xiao zhi bai bing.
       Laughter is the medicine to cure one hundred
       illnesses.

Xie   803   Hao xie bu cai chou gou si.
       Good shoes don't step in dog excrement.

Xin   804   Hai ren zhi xin bu ke you,
       fang ren zhi xin bu ke wu.
       Have the intent to harm no one, yet maintain
       a state of vigilance.

805   Jiao ren jiao xin, jiao hua jiao gen.
       Make friends heart to heart;
       water flowers at the root.

806   Jin xin shu bu ru bu du shu.
       If you believe everything you read, then
       you had better not read.

807   Lao xin zhe zhi ren, lao li zhe zhi yu ren.
Those who work with their brains rule and
those who work with their brawn are ruled.

808   Nu ren xin, hai di zhen.
A woman's heart is like a needle at the bottom
of the ocean.

809   Ren er wu xin, bu zhi qi ke?
If a man does not keep his word, what good is
he?

810   Ren tong xin, tu bian jin.
A meeting of minds can turn dirt into gold.

811   Ren xin gao guo tian,
zuo le huang di xiang cheng xian.
Desires are insatiable - ascend the throne as
emperor and you'll set your sights on
immortality.

812   Ren xin nan mo.
The human heart is difficult to grasp.

813   Ren xin yao gong, huo xin yao kong.
As the center of a fire needs air,
a person's heart needs to be fair.

814   San ren tong xin duo tian xia.
Three people of a common mind can conquer
the world.

815   Xin huan fan shao nian.
A joyous heart brings back youth.

816   Xin kuan ti pang.
       Broad mind, ample body.

817   Xin li tong kuai bai bing xiao.
       A joyous heart cures one hundred illnesses.

818   Xin zhong you shei, shei jiu piao liang.
       Whoever is in your heart is beautiful.

819   Yi xin bu neng er yong.
       One mind cannot be put to two uses.

Xing   820   Duo xing bu yi bi zi bi.
                   If one persists in doing unrighteous deeds, he is
                   bound to encounter an unfortunate end.

821   Fu qi he, jia wu xing; fu qi bu he, shui bu ning.
       When a couple get along, the home prospers;
       when a couple fight, they can't even get a good
       night's sleep.

822   Qian li zhi xing, shi yu zu xia.
       A journey of one thousand miles begins with a
       single step.

823   San ren xing bi you wo shi.
       When I walk in a group of three, among the
       others I may find a teacher for me.

824   Shu shui xing, hao hua chuan.
       If you know the nature of water, it is easier to
       row a boat.

825   Wen ji qi wu, bai shi ju xing.
       Start your day early and everything will
       prosper.

826　Xing bai li zhe ban jiu shi.
The going is toughest towards the end of a journey.

827　Xing dong sheng yu kong tan.
Action speaks louder than words.

Xiong　828　Qin xiong di, ming suan zhang.
Even brothers must settle accounts.

829　Xiong di bu he lin li qi,
jiang xiang bu mu lin guo qi.
Brothers who can't get along will be attacked by neighbors; generals who can't get along will be attacked by neighboring countries.

830　Xiong di bu he ying guo tie.
Brothers who don't get along are harder than iron.

831　Xiong di xi yu qiang, wai yu qi wu.
Brothers quarreling at home join forces against outside attacks.
Internal strife disappears in the face of external threat.

Xiu　832　Bu wei bu zhi er xiu, yao wei bu xue er kui.
Be ashamed for not learning rather than for not knowing.

833　Xiu cai bu chu men, neng zhi tian xia shi.
The learned need not leave their homes to know the world.

834 Xiu cai e si bu mai shu,
zhuang shi qiong si bu mai yi.
The scholar will not sell his books though in
extreme poverty, and the warrior will not
stoop to street performances.

Xu

835 Qian xu bu ru yi shi.
One thousand falsehoods are not as good as
one truth.

836 Xun xu jian jin, wu ye bu cheng.
Follow proper procedures and enjoy success in
whatever you do.

837 Yi ren chuan xu, wan ren chuan shi.
One man spreads a falsehood, and a multitude
passes it along as truth.

Xue

838 Bian xue bian wen, cai you xue wen.
Study and inquiry are the path to knowledge.

839 Bu ru hu xue, yan de hu zi.
You can't catch a tiger cub unless you go to
the tiger's lair.
Nothing ventured, nothing gained.

840 Gen ren zi sao men qian xue,
mo guan ta ren wa shang shuang.
Sweep the snow on your own doorstep and
ignore the frost on your neighbor's roof.
Mind your own business.

841 Gen shen me ren xue shen me yang,
gen zhe tu fu xue bu cheng pi jiang.
What you learn depends upon whom you
study with; if you study with a butcher, you
won't learn how to be a cobbler.

842   Ren bu xue, bu zhi yi.
      You must study to know what is righteous.

843   Xue bu yan lao.
      You are never too old to study.

844   Xue bu zhi qian, yi bi you xian.
      Learning without modesty limits one's skills.

845   Xue er bu si ze wang, si er bu xue ze dai.
      It is deceptive to study without reflection;
      it is dangerous to reflect without studying.

846   Xue pa yi zhi ban jie,
      fan pa ban sheng bu shou.
      Knowledge that is not assimilated is like half-
      cooked rice.

847   Xue ru ni shui xing zhou, bu jin ze tui.
      Learning is like paddling a canoe against the
      current - you will regress if you don't advance.

848   Xue wu lao shao, neng zhe wei shi.
      In the area of learning, age makes no difference;
      those who know will be the teacher.

849   Xue wu zhi jing.
      There is no limit to learning.

850   Xue xi ru gan lu, bu neng xie yi bu.
      Learning is like a rapid journey - you can't
      pause for even a moment.

Xuan   851   Hui xuan de xuan er lang,
                         bu hui xuan de xuan jia dang.
                         Those who know how will choose the son-in-
                         law; those who don't know how will choose
                         property.

Y

Yan

852   Bu ting lao ren yan, chi ku zai yan qian.
Listen to the words of your elders, or you will quickly regret it.

853   Duo yan re huo.
Less said, sooner mended.

854   Hong yan duo bo ming.
The fairest flowers soonest fade.

855   Jin zheng yan, man zhang kou.
Keep your eyes wide open, but open your mouth slowly.

856   Kuai ren yi yan, kuai ma yi bian.
A few words to the wise will suffice.

857   Liang yan ru er san dong nuan,
e yan shang ren liu yue han.
Good words warm a person up for three winters, while bad words chill the heart even in the heat of summer.

858   Qiao yan ling se xian yu ren.
          Full of courtesy, full of craft.

859   Ren zai ai yan xia, bu ke bu di tou.
          If you are standing under the eaves,
          you have to duck your head.

860   Yan bi xin, xing bi guo.
          Promises must be kept and action must be
          resolute.

861   Yan bu jian wei jing.
          Out of sight, out of mind.

862   Yan bu jian, xin bu fan.
          Out of sight, out of mind.

863   Yan duo bi shi.
          One is bound to have a slip of tongue if he
          talks too much.

864   Yan shi ai, song shi hai,
          bu guan bu jiao yao bian huai.
          Spare the rod and spoil the child.

865   Yan xie xin bu zheng, bi wai yi bu duan.
          Shifty eyes, shifty heart;
          crooked nose, crooked mind.

866   Yan yi lu ji, kuan yi dai ren.
          Be strict with oneself and broad-minded
          toward others.

867   Yi yan ji chu, si ma nan zhui.
          A word once spoken can't be retrieved even by
          a team of four horses.
          What is said can't be unsaid.

Yang   868   Wang yang bu lao, you wei wei wan.
It is not too late to mend the fence even if some
of the sheep have already escaped.
Better late than never.

869   Yang yang tong, yang yang song.
Jack of all trades, master of none.

Yao   870   Dui zheng xia yao, yao dao bing chu.
Administer medicine according to the diagnosis
and it will take effect immediately.

871   Liang yao ku kou, zhong yan ni er.
Just as bitter medicine cures sickness, so
unpalatable advice benefits conduct.

872   Yao bu bu ru shi bu.
Healthy food cures better than medicine.

Ye   873   Chuang ye nan, shou cheng geng nan.
It is difficult to start an undertaking, but
it is more difficult to maintain it.

874   Qian qiu da ye, fei yi ri zhi gong.
An enormous undertaking can't be
accomplished in one day.

875   Ye jing yu qin, huang yu xi.
In any undertaking, diligence leads to mastery,
while frivolity leads to decay.

Yi   876   Bu pa ren bu qing, jiu pa yi bu jing.
Be more concerned about your lack of skills
than the absence of an employer.

877   Jian yi si qian ye nan cheng.
You can't succeed if you often change course.

878 Jie lai de yi shang bu he ti.
Borrowed clothes don't fit well.

879 Kai juan you yi.
Read and reap the rewards.

880 Min yi bu ke wu.
Public opinion cannot be coerced.

881 Niao gui you yi, ren gui you zhi.
Wings are essential to a bird;
ambition is essential to a man.

882 Yi gao ren dan da.
Boldness of execution stems from superb skill.

883 Yi ren mo yong, yong ren mo yi.
Do not employ people you have doubts about,
and do not entertain doubts about the people
you employ.

884 Yi shang chang le ban tui,
xin yan duo le shou lei.
Clothes that are too long will trip you, as a
mind that is full of unnecessary misgivings
will vex you.

885 Yi xin sheng an gui.
Suspicions create imaginary fears.

886 Yi yi bang shen, zhong shen shou yong.
Possess a single skill, and reap the benefits
your whole life.

Yin 887 Dan xian bu cheng yin.
You can't make music with a single string.

888   Yin yuan ke yu bu ke qiu.
        Marital bliss arises spontaneously; it can't be
        sought after.

889   Yin yuan tian zhu ding.
        Marital bliss is predetermined by Heaven.

Ying   890   Bu yi cheng bai lun ying xiong.
                     You can't judge a hero by whether he wins or
                     loses.

891   Ying xiong bu pa chu shen di.
        Humble origins trouble not the hero.

892   Ying xiong nan guo mei ren guan.
        Even heroes find it hard to resist beauty.

893   Ying xiong suo jian lue tong.
        Great minds think alike.

894   Ying xiong you lei bu qing tan.
        Heroes fight back their tears.

895   Zhi fu meng hu fei ying xiong,
        yi zhu pi qi zhen hao han.
        The true hero is not one who can subdue a
        vicious tiger, but rather one who can restrain
        his own temper.

You   896   Gu you sheng xin zhi.
                    Old friends are better than new acquaintances.

897   Jiao you fen hou bo, chuan yi kan han shu.
        Distinguish between close and distant friends,
        as between summer and winter clothes.

898 Ren dao zhong nian wan shi you.
When people reach middle-age, they tend to worry a lot.

899 You yu wang shen.
Worry will ruin a man.
Care killed the cat.

Yu 900 Bai ri lian yin yu, zong you yi zhao qing.
A long spell of clouds and rain will be followed by a sunny day.

901 Chi li wu yu xia wei da,
shan zhong wu hu hou wei wang.
When there are no fish in the pond, the shrimp are in charge; when there are no tigers on the mountain, the monkey is king.

902 Chun yu gui ru you.
Rain in spring is as precious as oil.

903 Fan shi yu ze li, bu yu ze fei.
Come prepared and succeed;
come unprepared and fail.

904 Ji yu chen zhou.
Enough feathers can sink a boat.

905 Ning wei yu sui, bu wei wa quan.
Better to be a broken piece of jade than an intact roofing tile.
Better to die in glory than survive with dishonor.

906 Tan shi yu er yi shang gou.
The fish will soon be caught that nibbles at every lure.

907 Wei yu chou mou.
Repair the roof before it rains.
Make hay while the sun shines.

908 Xiao yu jiu xia neng cheng zai.
Frequent drizzle can cause floods.

909 Yu bu neng xia yi nian,
ren bu neng qiong yi bei.
Rain will not fall all year long, and people
will not be poor throughout their lives.

910 Yu bu zhuo, bu cheng qi.
If jade is not cut and polished, it can't be
made into anything.

911 Yu fang sheng yu zhi liao.
Prevention is better than cure.

912 Yu zhe qian lu, bi you yi de.
Even a fool occasionally hits on a good idea.

913 Zhua yu yao xia shui, fa mu yao ru lin.
You have to go to sea to catch fish, and
you have to go to the forest to cut wood.

Yuan   914 Bu shi yuan jia bu ju tou.
Enemies and lovers are destined to meet.

915 Ning zou shi bu yuan, bu zou yi bu xian.
Better to take ten safe steps than a single
dangerous one.
Better safe than sorry.

916 Xing yuan bi zi er.
The road to greatness begins at home.

917 Yin shui yao si yuan, wei ren bu wang ben.
When drinking water, think of the source;
when living your life, remember who you are.

918 You yuan qian li lai xiang hui,
wu yuan dui mian bu xiang shi.
Fate will bring two people together though
they are separated by one thousand miles;
fate will prevent two people from meeting
though they are standing face to face.

919 Yuan chou yi jie bu yi jie.
Better to resolve enmity than to create it.

920 Yuan chu zhuo yan, jin chu zhuo shou.
Set long-term goals, but work on short-term
tasks.

921 Yuan jia lu zai.
The road of enemies is narrow; they will surely
to meet. One can't avoid one's enemy.

922 Yuan you tou, zhai you zhu.
Put the saddle on the right horse.

Yue 923 Du yue le, bu ru zhong yue le.
Music is best enjoyed with others.

924 Ri zhong ze ze, yue ying ze shi.
The moon waxes, and then it wanes.

925 Yue er wan wan, zhao jiu zhou,
ji jia huan le ji jia chou.
When the crescent moon shines over China,
some families are happy and others are sad.

Yun   926   Tian shang wu yun bu xia yu,
                          shi jian wu li shi bu cheng.
                          No clouds, no rain; no rules, no gain.

                 927   Yun bu ju ji yu bu xia, ren bu tuan jie li bu da.
                          If the clouds don't form, there will be no rain;
                          if people don't unite, they will have no power.

Z

Zai	928	Qian zai de duo jian wang,

Zai   928   Qian zai de duo jian wang,
tao zai de ji xing qiang.
Debtors have short memories, while creditors
have long memories.

Zei   929   Zuo zei yue lao yue dan xiao.
The older the thief, the more cowardly.

Zhai   930   Wu zhai yi shen qing.
Out of debt, out of danger.

Zhang   931   Ren yao chang jiao, zhang yao duan jie.
Friendship should be long-lived, while
debts should be short-lived.

Zhao   932   Yi zhao bu shen, man pan jie shu.
One careless chess move, and the game is lost.

Zhen   933   Lin zhen mo dao wan.
It is too late to sharpen your sword on the
brink of battle.

934   Wu zhen bu yin xian, wu shui bu xing chuan.
You don't pull thread without a needle;
you don't row a boat without water.

935 Xing jia you ru zhen tiao tu,
bai jia hao si shui tui zhou.
To bring prosperity to a family is as difficult
as carrying dirt with a needle; to lead a family
to ruin is as easy as casting a boat downstream.

936 Yi zhen bu bu, qian zhen nan feng.
A stitch in time saves nine.

937 Yi zhi zhen wu liang tou li.
A single needle has only one point.

938 Zhi yao gong fu shen, tie chi mo cheng zhen.
If you work at it hard enough, you can grind
an iron rod down to a needle.

Zheng 939 Ji shen zheng, bu ling er xing.
We reform others unconsciously when we act
righteously.

940 Li zheng bu que fa.
Those who are upright fear not the law.

941 Ren zheng yi kou qi, fou zheng yi zhu xiang.
Men strive for vindication; God strives for
manifestation.

942 Shen zheng bu pa ying er xie.
The upright man is not concerned that his
shadow is crooked.

943 Xin bu zheng, xing bu wen.
The man of low integrity travels a rocky road.

944 Xin zheng bu pa xie.
Evil will not harm a person of integrity.

Zhi

945 Yi ren xin bu zheng, xin zheng bu yi ren.
A suspicious person is not upright, and an
upright person has no suspicions.

946 Yi zheng liang chou, yi rang liang you.
One fight sullies two persons; one compromise
benefits two persons.

947 Yu bang xiang zheng, yu weng de li.
When the snipe and the clam fight, the
fisherman wins. It is the third party that
benefits from a struggle.

948 Bu pa zhi duan, jiu pa zhi duan.
Be more concerned about lofty aspirations
than limited knowledge.

949 Chuan dao qiao tou zi ran zhi.
Everything will work out in the end.

950 Da zhi ruo yu.
A man of great wisdom often appears slow-
witted. Still waters run deep.

951 Hao han ping zhi qiang,
huo ma ping dan zhuang.
Great men rely on great ambition, as good
horses rely on courage.

952 Jian le zhi ma diu le xi gua.
Pick up the sesame seeds but overlook the
watermelons.
Penny wise and pound foolish.

953 Ren gui you zhi, xue gui you heng.
High aspirations are essential for a man,
as persistence is essential for learning.

954 Ren ping zhi qi hu ping wei.
A man is defined by his ambitions,
as a tiger by his strength.

955 Ren qiong zhi duan.
Poverty stifles ambition.

956 Ren sheng wu zhi, ru wu duo zhi zhou.
Living without aspirations is like a boat
without a helm.

957 Ren you zhi, zhu you jie.
Men have aspirations as bamboo has joints.

958 Ren zhi xiang zhi, gui zai zhi xin.
The most important thing in knowing another
is to know what lies in the heart.

959 Ruo yao ren bu zhi, chu fei ji mo wei.
The best way of not being caught is not to
commit the act. Murder will out.

960 Xiao zhi fang da die.
A stumble may prevent a fall.

961 You zhi bu zai nian gao.
With ambition, age matters not.

962 You zhi fu ren sheng guo nan zi.
Women with ambition are stronger than men.

963 You zhi piao yang guo hai,
wu zhi cun bu nan xing.
With aspirations you can go anywhere;
without aspirations you can go nowhere.

964 You zhi zhe shi jing cheng.
Where there is a will, there is a way.

965 Yu zhi xin fu shi, xian ting kou zhong yan.
If you wish to know what is in a person's
heart, listen first to what he says.

966 Zhi bao bu zhu huo.
You can't wrap fire in paper.
Truth will out.

967 Zhi ji zhi bi, bai zhan bai sheng.
Knowing both oneself and one's opponent is
the certain way to victory.

968 Zhi shi jiu shi li liang.
Knowledge is power.

969 Zhi shi yu qian, zi xin yu shen.
The more shallow the knowledge, the greater
the arrogance.

970 Zhi zhe bu yan, yan zhe bu zhi.
Those who know do not talk, and those who
talk do not know.

971 Zhi zhe gua yan, yu zhe duo zui.
The wise say little, while fools babble.

972 Zhi zhe qian lu, bi you yi shi.
Even the greatest men stumble.

973 Zhi zhi wei zhi zhi, bu zhi wei bu zhi,
shi zhi ye.
Admit what you know and what you don't
know - that is knowledge.

974 Zhi zhu qin zhi wang, zong you fei lai chong.
If a spider works hard spinning webs, it will
eventually catch insects.
Hard work will pay off.

975 Zhi zhu zhang wang hao tian qi.
Spider webs portend fine weather.

Zhong 976 Bu mo cheng gan, bu zhi tuo zhong.
You must shoulder a load to appreciate its
weight.

977 Jiang xiang ben wu zhong, nan er dang zi
qiang.
Masters are made, not born.

978 Zhong wei qing gen.
The heavy is the root of the light.

Zhu 979 Fu mu bu ke wei zhu, bei ren bu ke wei zhu.
Rotten wood is not used for pillars; scoundrels
do not become masters.

980 Hao zhu chu hao sun.
Good bamboo produces good bamboo shoots.
Good children come from good parents.

981 Jin zhu zhe chi, jin mo zhe hei.
He who handles vermilion will be reddened,
and he who touches ink will be blackened.
He who keeps company with the wolf will
learn to howl.

982 Yi gen zhu zi dong, gen gen wei liang yao.
The shifting of a single pillar will shake all of
the beams.

983 Yuan zhu xiang, jin zhu liang.
Live near and be far from the heart;
live far away and be near to the heart.

984 Zhu duo rou jian.
When pigs are plenty, pork is cheap.

Zhuan 985 Ren xin zhuan, shi shan chuan.
Maintain focus and you can bore through a mountain.

Zhuang 986 Ti zhuang ren qi bing, ti ruo ren bing qi.
The strong ward off disease, while the weak are stricken by disease.

Zi 987 Jiao zi cong xiao qi, zhi jia qin jian qi.
The education of children begins when they are little; the management of a household begins with industry and frugality.

988 Shao chi duo zi wei, duo chi huo shou zui.
Eat less and enjoy the taste more; eat more and enjoy your health less.

989 Si zi qian jin, bu ru si zi yi yi.
Better to impart a single skill upon a child than to bestow upon the child a thousand pieces of gold.

Zong 990 Zong er hai er, zong qi hai zi ji.
Spoil your child, harm your child;
spoil your wife, harm yourself.

Zu 991 Jie zu xian deng.
The early bird catches the worm.

992   Yi shi zu cheng qian gu hen.
One false step brings everlasting grief.
Short pleasure, long lament.

993   Yi shi zu ze zhi rong ru.
Honor and disgrace matter only to those who
have fulfilled their material needs.

994   Zhi zu chang le.
A contented mind is a perpetual feast.

Zui   995   Gou zui tu bu chu xiang ya.
A filthy mouth will not utter decent language.

996   Ren zui bu qian zhai.
If you limit your desires, you will avoid debts.

997   Ren zui ru qing cao, feng chui liang bian dao.
Our mouths are like grass and our words sway
with the prevailing wind.

998   Zui qiao duo shang feng.
The eloquent are at an advantage.

Zuo   999   Ning ke zuo guo, bu ke cuo guo.
Better to do it than to miss it.

1000   Zuo chi shan kong.
Sit idle and eat, and in time your whole
fortune will be used up.

Bibliography

Chinnery, John D. *Corresponding English and Chinese Proverbs and Phrases With Explanations and Examples*. Beijing: New World Press, 1984.

Cui, Mingqiu and Fowkes, S. W. *The Wisdom of the Chinese Proverbs*. Palo Alto: Bottom Books, 1990.

Diao Yu Weng 釣魚翁. *Miao Yu Ru Zhu* 妙語如珠 (Pearls of Wit). Taipei: Han Wei Chubanshe, 1986.

Feldman, Reynold and Voelke, Cynthia. *A World Treasury of Folk Wisdom*. Taipei: Yuanliu Chuban Shiye Co., Ltd., 1993.

Feng, Gia-fu (trans.) and English, Jane (trans.). *Chuang Tsu*. New York: Random House, 1974.

Feng, Gia-fu (trans.) and English, Jane (trans.). *Tao Te Ching*. New York: Random House, 1972.

Giles, Lionel (trans.). *The Book of Mencius* (abridged). Boston: Charles E. Tuttle Co., Inc., 1993.

Guan, Meifen 管梅芬. *Zhongguo Suyu Yu Yanyu* 中國俗語與諺語 (Chinese Sayings and Proverbs). Taipei: Wenguo Shuju, 1993.

Guan, Meifen 管梅芬. *Zhongguo Yanyu Xuanji* 中國諺語選輯 (Selected Chinese Proverbs). Taipei: Wenguo Shuju, 1993.

Hong, Jiahui 洪嘉惠. *Wo Bu Zai Yongcuo Yanyu* 我不再用錯諺語 (Proverbs I'll Never Use Incorrectly Again). Taipei: Mingren Chubanshe, 1979.

Legge, James (trans.). *The Four Books*. Taipei: Wenhua Tushu Co., 1979.

Liang, Shiqiu 梁實秋. *A New Practical Chinese-English Dictionary*. 最新實用漢英辭典 Taipei: The Far East Book Co., Ltd., 1983.

Lin, Yutang. *The Importance of Understanding*. Cleveland: The World Publishing Company, 1960.

Liu, Junwen 劉俊文 and Qin, Bixiao 秦畢嘯. *Zhongguo Minjian Suyu* 中國民間俗語 (Folk Adages of China). Taipei: Han Xi Wenhua Shiye Co., Ltd., 1995.

Plopper, Clifford H. *Chinese Proverbs: Economics As Seen Through the Proverbs.* Beijing: North China Union Language School, 1932.

Qi, Fei 飛飛. *Zhongguo Minjian Yanyu* 中國民間諺語 (Folk Proverbs of China). Taipei: Man Ting Fang Chubanshe, 1994.

Smith, Arthur. *Proverbs and Common Sayings From the Chinese.* New York: Paragon Book Reprint Co. (reprint), 1965.

Tian, Zongyao 田宗堯. *Zhongguo Gudian Xiaoshuo Yongyu Cidian* 中國古典小說用語辭典 (Dictionary of Phrases From Chinese Classical Novels). Taipei: Lianjing Chuban Shiye Co., 1985.

Tian, Zongyao 田宗堯. *Zhongguo Huaben Xiaoshuo Suyu Cidian* 中國話本小說俗語辭典 (A Dictionary of Colloquial Terms and Expression in Chinese Vernacular Novels). Taipei: Xin Wen Feng Chuban Co., Ltd., 1985.

Wang, Defu 王德富 et. al. *Hanyu Chengyu Yingyi Shouce* 漢語成語英譯手册 (A Handbook of Chinese Idioms With English Translation). Sichuan: Sichuan Renmin Chubanshe, 1980.

Wu, Jingrong 吳景榮. *The Chinese-English Dictionary* 漢英辭典. Beijing: The Commercial Press, Ltd., 1978.

Zeng, Yuanpei 曾淵培 et. al. *Wen Shin English-Chinese Dictionary of Contemporary English* 文馨當代英漢辭典. Taipei: Wen Shin Publishing Co., 1985.

English Key Word Index

Index entries are arranged by *key word*, by which is meant the single English word most closely associated with the meaning and significance of the proverb. In most cases, the English key word corresponds directly to the Chinese key word for a given proverb. All numbers refer to the numbered Chinese proverb entries.

Chinese Appendix

1. 哀莫大於心死.
2. 愛屋及烏.
3. 愛要細水長流.
4. 惜花花結果, 愛柳柳成蔭.
5. 居安思危.
6. 驕傲是成功的敵人.
7. 一個巴掌拍不響.
8. 東家不敗落, 西家不發作.
9. 行要好子伴, 住要好鄰.
10. 飽漢不知餓漢飢.
11. 豹死留皮, 人死留名.
12. 鄰舍好, 無價寶.
13. 善惡到頭終有報, 遠走高飛也難逃.
14. 善有善報, 惡有惡報.
15. 易求無價寶, 難得有情郎

16. 悖入悖出.

17. 登高必自卑.

18. 人比人，氣死人.

19. 扁擔沒扎，兩頭打塌.

20. 苦海無邊，回頭是岸.

21. 七十二變，本相難變.

22. 雄辯是銀，沉默是金.

23. 小別勝新婚.

24. 哀兵必勝.

25. 兵不離陣，虎不離山.

26. 兵不厭詐.

27. 病從口入，禍從口出.

28. 冰凍三尺，非一日之寒.

29. 兵貴精，不貴多.

30. 兵貴神速，人貴鬼索.

31. 病好不謝醫，下次沒人醫.

32. 病急亂投醫.

33. 兵隨將相草隨風.

34. 急病在治，慢病在養.

35. 驕兵必敗.
36. 久病成良醫.
37. 久病無孝子.
38. 同病相憐.
39. 養兵千日, 用兵一時.
40. 有病才知健是仙.
41. 有病早治, 省錢省事.
42. 財多不露, 藝高不顯; 愛露愛顯, 必有風險.
43. 財多累身, 慾多傷神.
44. 財多招賊, 人俊招邪.
45. 買了便宜柴, 燒爛夾底鍋.
46. 親雖親, 財帛分.
47. 青柴難燒, 嬌子難教.
48. 人為財死, 鳥為食亡.
49. 天生我材必有用.
50. 勿貪竟外之財.
51. 小財不出, 大財不入.
52. 曾經滄海難為水.

53. 操心易老.

54. 三十六策, 走為上策.

55. 差之毫釐, 謬以千里.

56. 好茶不怕細品, 好事不怕細論.

57. 寧喝朋友的淡茶, 不喝敵人的蜜酒.

58. 有恆產, 不如有恆心.

59. 常說口裡順, 常做手不笨.

60. 取人之長, 補己之短.

61. 覆巢之下無完卵.

62. 車到山前必有路.

63. 前車之覆, 後車之鑒.

64. 不怕學不成, 就怕心不誠.

65. 成功是三分天才七分努力.

66. 精誠所至, 金石為開.

67. 巧詐不如拙誠.

68. 一人難稱百人意.

69. 吃虧就是佔便宜.

70. 貨問三家不吃虧.

71. 醜人愛戴花.

72. 醜人愛作怪.

73. 夫妻吵嘴不記仇.

74. 家醜不可外揚.

75. 流水不臭, 臭水不流.

76. 人死不記仇.

77. 天天不發愁, 活到百出頭.

78. 無丑不成戲.

79. 一醉解千愁, 醒後還在愁.

80. 廚子多胖子.

81. 羊毛出在羊身上.

82. 百川歸海.

83. 船大吃水深.

84. 船到江心補漏遲.

85. 後上船者先上岸.

86. 小船不宜重載.

87. 常開窗, 保健康.

88. 慈不掌兵, 義不掌財.

89. 聰明保一人, 富貴保一家.

90. 聰明反被聰明誤.

91. 聰明人也會做傻事.
92. 醋是陳的酸.
93. 為人不怕錯, 就怕不改過.
94. 不打不成器.
95. 不打不相識.
96. 打是疼, 罵是愛.
97. 不挑擔子不知重, 不走長路不知遠.
98. 膽小做不得將軍.
99. 看人挑擔不吃力.
100. 正擔好挑, 偏擔難挨.
101. 不上當, 不成內行.
102. 頭回上當, 二回心亮.
103. 刀槍不認人.
104. 得道多助, 失道寡助.
105. 放下屠刀, 立地成佛.
106. 君子謀道不謀食.
107. 夜盜恨明月.
108. 一人得道, 雞犬升天.
109. 得不足喜, 失不足憂.

110. 上德不德，是以有德．
111. 黄河有底，人心無底．
112. 涓涓之滴，滙成江河．
113. 千里之堤，潰于蟻穴．
114. 自己跌倒自己爬．
115. 不經冬寒，哪知春暖．
116. 冬不節約春要愁，夏不勞動秋無收．
117. 隆冬之後必有陽春．
118. 不賭是嬴几钱．
119. 初生之犢不畏虎．
120. 隔層肚皮隔重山．
121. 惡不積，不足以喪身．
122. 惡人先告狀．
123. 積惡者喪．
124. 萬惡皆由自私起．
125. 一人作惡，千人遭殃．
126. 要知父母恩，懷裡抱兒孫．
127. 一夜夫妻百日恩．
128. 愛兒當訓子．

129. 兒不嫌母醜, 狗不嫌主貧.

130. 兒大不由爺, 女大不由娘.

131. 兒行千里母擔憂.

132. 小兒無詐病.

133. 一耳好睹, 眾目難掩.

134. 王子犯法, 與民同罪.

135. 按人口做飯, 量身體裁衣.

136. 飯後百步走, 活到九十九.

137. 飯莫不嚼便吞, 話莫不想就說.

138. 煩惱不尋人, 人自尋煩惱.

139. 凡事起頭難, 做了就不難.

140. 今日且吃今日飯, 明天有事明天辦.

141. 冷粥冷飯好吃, 冷言冷語難受.

142. 寧可吃錯飯, 不可說錯話.

143. 向陽房子先得暖, 靠水人家會撐船.

144. 予人方便, 自己方便.

145. 百里不同風.

146. 逢人只說三分話.

147. 疾風知勁草.

148. 逆風點火自燒身.
149. 三年風水輪流轉.
150. 山雨欲來風滿樓.
151. 順風吹火, 用力不多.
152. 無風不起浪.
153. 醜婦家中寶.
154. 大富由天, 小富由儉.
155. 大丈夫能屈能伸.
156. 夫唱婦隨.
157. 富貴好, 不如兒孫好.
158. 福無雙至.
159. 虎父無犬子.
160. 禍福為鄰.
161. 禍兮福所倚, 福兮禍所伏.
162. 貧賤夫妻百事哀.
163. 巧婦難為無米之炊.
164. 饒人是福.
165. 塞翁失馬, 焉知非福.
166. 身在福中不知福.

167. 天下無不是的父母.

168. 一分度量一分福, 能忍便是有福人.

169. 庸人多厚福.

170. 有其父, 必有其子.

171. 多深的根基, 築多高的牆.

172. 樹靠根, 屋靠梁.

173. 斬草不除根, 春風吹又生.

174. 功到自然成.

175. 工欲善其事, 必先利其器.

176. 好鬥的公雞不長毛.

177. 開弓沒有回頭箭.

178. 慢弓出細活.

179. 無功不受祿.

180. 一日讀書一日功, 一日不讀十日空.

181. 做事不依歌, 累死也無功.

182. 打狗看主人.

183. 大狗爬牆, 小狗看樣.

184. 狗急跳牆.

185. 好狗不擋道.

186. 好狗不咬鷄，好漢不打妻．
187. 會叫的狗不會咬人．
188. 老狗學不來新花樣．
189. 天晴不開溝，雨落遍地流．
190. 咬人狗，不露齒．
191. 德不孤，必有鄰．
192. 鼓不敲不響，理不辯不明．
193. 鼓空則聲高，人狂則話大．
194. 寡婦門前是非多．
195. 寡酒難喝，寡婦難熬．
196. 種瓜得瓜，種豆得豆．
197. 見怪不怪，其怪自敗．
198. 打了三年官司，當得半個律師．
199. 清官難斷家務事．
200. 無官一身輕．
201. 新官不管舊事．
202. 新官上任三把火．
203. 光陰容易過，歲月莫蹉跎．
204. 光陰如流水，一去不復回．

205. 光陰似箭.
206. 一寸光陰一寸金, 寸金難買寸光陰.
207. 貴人多忘事.
208. 常思己過, 免於招禍.
209. 過而不改, 是為過矣.
210. 過而能改, 善莫大焉.
211. 國家興亡, 匹夫有責.
212. 國以民為本, 民以食為天.
213. 過猶不及.
214. 國之本在家, 家之本在身.
215. 買鍋要敲打, 娶嫁要細查.
216. 蛤蟆有時也會被泥陷住.
217. 海水不可斗量.
218. 窮人的孩子早當家.
219. 四海之內皆兄弟.
220. 有媽的孩子像個寶, 沒娘的孩子像根草.
221. 好漢不吃眼前虧.
222. 好漢做事好漢當.

223. 男子漢大丈夫,不為五斗米折腰.

224. 若非一番寒徹骨,焉得梅花撲鼻香.

225. 行行出狀元.

226. 行行有利,行行有弊.

227. 男怕入錯行,女怕嫁錯郎.

228. 同行是冤家.

229. 同行相嫉.

230. 做一行,怨一行,到老不在行.

231. 好人不長壽,壞人活百年.

232. 好事不過三.

233. 好事多磨.

234. 光頭不一定是和尚.

235. 河裏淹死會水人.

236. 和氣生財.

237. 河有兩岸,事有兩面.

238. 家和萬事興.

239. 懶和尚做不出好齋來.

240. 外來的和尚會唸經.

241. 小河溝也能翻船.

242. 想要過河先搭橋.

243. 一個和尚挑水喝,兩個和尚擡水喝,
三個和尚沒水喝.

244. 做一日和尚, 撞一日鐘.

245. 人有恆心萬事成.

246. 虎毒不食子.

247. 畫虎畫皮難畫骨, 知人知面不知心.

248. 老虎也有打盹時.

249. 兩虎相爭, 必有一傷.

250. 上山擒虎易, 開口求人難.

251. 多吃無滋味, 多話不值錢.

252. 方話難入圓耳朵.

253. 好話三遍, 連狗都嫌.

254. 好看的花兒未必香.

255. 話不投機半句多.

256. 話不要說死, 話不要走絕.

257. 話多不甜, 膠多不黏.

258. 話多了傷人, 食多了傷身.

259. 花美美一時, 人美美一世.

260. 花有重開日，人無再少年。

261. 看花容易繡花難。

262. 老虎花在背，人心花在內。

263. 聽小話，誤大事。

264. 不貴難得之貨，使民不為盜。

265. 不貪財，禍不來。

266. 闖禍容易消災難。

267. 蓋得住火，藏不住煙。

268. 好貨不怕試，怕試沒好貨。

269. 好貨不便宜，便宜無好貨。

270. 禍不單行。

271. 禍福無門，唯人自招。

272. 禍福自取。

273. 火急炻不好餅，火猛燒不好飯。

274. 禍難入慎家之門。

275. 虧心人是禍。

276. 煉鐵需要烈火，交友需要誠心。

277. 烈火見純金。

278. 星星之火可以燎原。

279. 野火燒不盡, 春風吹又生.

280. 不吃飯則飢, 不讀書則愚.

281. 大雞不食細米.

282. 好記性不如爛筆頭.

283. 黃鼠狼給雞拜年, 沒安好心.

284. 飢不擇食.

285. 雞肚那知鴨肚.

286. 雞肥不下蛋.

287. 積絲成縷, 積寸成尺.

288. 見機行事.

289. 寧做雞頭, 不做牛後.

290. 心急吃不得熱粥.

291. 一年之計在於春, 一日之計在於晨.

292. 不當家, 不知柴米貴; 不生子, 不知父田恩.

293. 當家才知柴米貴, 出門才曉路難行.

294. 家不知, 外人欺.

295. 家家有本難唸的經.

296. 家裡有個節約手, 一年吃穿都不愁.

297. 鄰家失火, 不救自危.

298. 你看我家好, 我看你家好.
299. 成見不可有, 定見不可無.
300. 豐年儉 災年足.
301. 利箭還要靠強弓.
302. 無奸不顯忠.
303. 由儉入奢易, 由奢入儉難.
304. 不怕浪頭高, 就怕槳不齊.
305. 好將不說當年勇.
306. 薑是老的辣.
307. 精工匠不如巧主人.
308. 良匠無棄材.
309. 強將手下無弱兵.
310. 三個臭皮匠, 勝過一個諸葛亮.
311. 一個好皮匠, 沒有好鞋樣;
     二個笨皮匠, 做事好商量.
312. 不濕腳的人捕不到魚.
313. 不細嚼, 不知味.
314. 交淺不可言深.
315. 君子之交淡如水.

316. 請教別人不吃虧.

317. 貪多嚼不爛.

318. 細嚼慢嚥, 壽活百年.

319. 節約好比燕銜泥, 浪費好比河決堤.

320. 每逢佳節倍思親.

321. 行船靠掌舵, 理家靠節約.

322. 有借有還, 再借不難.

323. 家有千金, 不及日進分文.

324. 謹開口, 慢許諾.

325. 金憑火鍊, 人憑心交.

326. 金玉滿堂, 莫之能守.

327. 寧捨一塊金, 不捨一句春.

328. 遍地皆黃金, 專等勤苦人.

329. 千金難買心頭願.

330. 失落寸金容易找, 錯過光陰無處尋.

331. 真金不怕火鍊.

332. 好景不常在.

333. 你敬友人一寸, 人敬你一丈.

334. 入境隨俗.

335. 心靜自然涼.

336. 一動不如一靜.

337. 一人開井, 千家飲水.

338. 舊的不去, 新的不來.

339. 酒後吐真言.

340. 酒能成事, 酒能敗事.

341. 青酒紅人面, 財帛動人心.

342. 當局者迷, 旁觀者清.

343. 好聚不如好散.

344. 處君子易, 處小人難.

345. 君子報仇, 十年不晚.

346. 君子不失赤子之心.

347. 君子有成人之美.

348. 能言不是真君子, 善處才是大丈夫.

349. 養軍如養虎, 虎大必傷人.

350. 只給君子看門, 不給小人當家.

351. 好的開始是成功的一半.

352. 靠人都是假, 跌倒自己爬.

353. 一刻千金.

354. 相罵無好口, 相打無好手.

355. 不嚐黃連苦, 哪知蜂蜜甜.

356. 吃得苦中苦, 方為人上人.

357. 苦盡甘來.

358. 人生最苦老來孤.

359. 先苦後甘, 富貴萬年.

360. 老王賣瓜, 自賣自誇.

361. 助人為快樂之本.

362. 白日不做虧心事, 半夜不怕鬼敲門.

363. 吃一回虧, 學一回乖.

364. 好來不如好去.

365. 來而不往非禮也.

366. 只有懶人, 沒有懶地.

367. 長江後浪推前浪, 一代更比一代強.

368. 浪子回頭金不換.

369. 不怕人老, 只怕心老.

370. 活到老, 學到老.

371. 家中有一老, 好似有一寶.

372. 老人休娶少年妻.

313. 人老疑心重.
314. 十老九病.
315. 樹老根多, 人老識多.
316. 樂極生悲.
317. 雷聲大, 雨點小.
318. 天冷不凍忙人.
319. 薄利多銷生意好.
320. 公理勝強權.
321. 公說公有理, 婆說婆有理.
322. 故有之以為利, 無之以為用.
323. 婚禮鋪張, 兩敗俱傷.
324. 理不辯不明, 話不講不清.
325. 禮多必詐.
326. 利潤大, 風險大.
327. 理治好人, 法制壞人.
328. 寧吃好梨一個, 不吃爛梨一筐.
329. 一理通, 百理明.
330. 一時強弱在於力, 古勝負在於理.
331. 有理不在聲高.

373. 人老疑心重.
374. 十老九病.
375. 樹老根多, 人老識多.
376. 樂極生悲.
377. 雷聲大, 雨點小.
378. 天冷不凍忙人.
379. 薄利多銷生意好.
380. 公理勝強權.
381. 公說公有理, 婆說婆有理.
382. 故有之以為利, 無之以為用.
383. 婚禮鋪張, 兩敗俱傷.
384. 理不辯不明, 話不講不清.
385. 禮多必詐.
386. 利潤大, 風險大.
387. 理治好人, 法制壞人.
388. 寧吃好梨一個, 不吃爛梨一筐.
389. 一理通, 百理明.
390. 一時強弱在於力, 古勝負在於理.
391. 有理不在聲高.

392. 有理走遍天下，無理寸步難行．

393. 有一利必有一弊．

394. 真理愈辯愈明．

395. 一天不練手腳慢，兩天不練去一半．

396. 會打會算，糧食不斷．

397. 買屋看梁，娶妻看娘．

398. 上梁不正，下梁歪．

399. 仙丹難治沒良心．

400. 聊勝於無．

401. 獨木不成林．

402. 近鄰不可斷，遠友不可疏．

403. 解鈴還需繫鈴人．

404. 困龍也有上天時．

405. 龍生龍，鳳生鳳，耗子生來會打洞．

406. 龍游淺水遭蝦戲，虎落平陽被犬欺．

407. 擒龍要下海，打虎要上山．

408. 要吃龍肉，自己下海．

409. 補漏趁天晴，讀書趁年輕．

410. 萬丈高樓平地起！

411. 不怕路長, 只怕志短.
412. 常問路不迷.
413. 大路有千條, 真理只一條.
414. 路是走熟的, 事是做順的.
415. 路遙知馬力, 日久見人心.
416. 人無遠慮, 必有近憂.
417. 人行千里路, 勝讀十年書.
418. 事不經不懂, 路不走不平.
419. 天無絕人之路.
420. 一人修路, 萬人安步.
421. 走盡崎嶇路, 自有平坦途.
422. 別自找麻煩.
423. 常驚不驚, 常打不靈.
424. 好馬不吃回頭草.
425. 好馬不停蹄, 好牛不停犁.
426. 老馬識途.
427. 馬好不在叫, 人美不在貌.
428. 馬靠鞍裝, 人靠衣裝.
429. 馬老識路途, 人老通世故.

430. 麻雀雖小, 五臟俱全.

431. 螞蟻搬家, 大雨將下.

432. 又要馬兒跑得快, 又要馬兒不吃草.

433. 院子裡跑不出千里馬.

434. 買盡天下物, 難買子孫賢.

435. 慢步跌不倒, 小心錯不了.

436. 滿招損, 謙受益.

437. 好叫的貓逮不住老鼠.

438. 懶貓逮不住死老鼠.

439. 貓苗發威也成不了老虎.

440. 美貌是全能, 金錢是萬能.

441. 那個貓兒不吃老鼠.

442. 人不可貌相.

443. 外貌容易認, 內心最難猜.

444. 嘴上無毛, 辦事不牢.

445. 十個媒婆九個謊.

446. 出門看天色, 買賣看行情.

447. 豪門多孽子.

448. 夢隨心生.

449. 百密也有一疏.
450. 生米煮成熟飯.
451. 一樣米養百樣人.
452. 不識盧山真面目,只緣身在此山中.
453. 到什麼廟,燒什麼香.
454. 民以食為天.
455. 不怕生壞命,就怕生壞病.
456. 兼聽則明,偏信則暗.
457. 美名難得而易失.
458. 名可名非常名.
459. 名利二字是非多.
460. 明人不做暗事.
461. 明照暗事,理服人心.
462. 人過留名,雁過留聲.
463. 人怕出名,豬怕壯.
464. 將在謀而不在勇,兵在精而不在多.
465. 獨木不成林.
466. 剛木易折,強弓易斷.
467. 嚴霜見真木.

468. 有奶便是娘.

469. 患難見真情.

470. 天下無難事, 只怕有心人.

471. 能者多勞.

472. 勤娘常出懶兒子.

473. 鳥之將死, 其鳴也哀; 人之將死, 其言也善.

474. 寧為屋上鳥, 不做房裡妾.

475. 一鳥在手, 勝過百鳥在林.

476. 老牛好使.

477. 牛大壓不了蝨子.

478. 歡場女兒真無情.

479. 寧犯天公怒, 莫犯眾人惱.

480. 女大十八變.

481. 女大十八一枝花.

482. 忍一時之怒, 可免百日之憂.

483. 盛怒之下識為人.

484. 小人物易發怒.

485. 眾怒難犯.

486. 爬得高, 跌得重.
487. 一口吃不成個胖子.
488. 酒肉朋友好找, 患難之交難縫.
489. 否極泰來.
490. 皮之不存, 毛將焉附.
491. 口說無憑, 事實為證.
492. 滿瓶不響, 半瓶晃盪.
493. 人平不語, 水平不流.
494. 久住坡, 不嫌陡.
495. 婆有德, 媳婦賢.
496. 家有賢妻, 夫有閒逸.
497. 氣大傷神, 食大傷身.
498. 乞丐無種, 懶漢自成.
499. 氣可鼓而不可洩.
500. 器小易盈.
501. 企者不立.
502. 娶妻求淑女.
503. 娶妻娶德不娶色.
504. 人爭氣, 火爭焰.

505. 正氣高, 邪氣消.

506. 被犬所吠者, 未必皆盜竊.

507. 吃一塹, 長一智.

508. 到處不用錢, 處處惹人嫌.

509. 酒肉朋友, 沒錢分手.

510. 錢財身外物.

511. 錢財越花越少, 知識越學越多.

512. 錢到公事辦, 火到豬頭爛.

513. 錢到光棍手, 一去一回頭.

514. 錢能通神.

515. 前人種樹, 後人乘涼.

516. 前事不忘, 後事之師.

517. 謙虛是成功的朋友.

518. 人賺錢難, 錢賺錢容易.

519. 無錢不成事.

520. 瞎子見錢眼睛開.

521. 一分錢, 一分貨.

522. 一犬吠形, 百犬吠聲.

523. 用人錢財, 替人消災.

524. 有錢勤事稱心意.
525. 有錢常想無錢日, 豐年常記大荒年.
526. 有錢蓋百醜.
527. 有錢難買後悔藥.
528. 有錢難買少年時.
529. 有錢能使鬼推磨.
530. 有錢一條龍, 無錢一條蟲.
531. 折東牆, 補西牆, 結果還是住破房.
532. 隔牆有耳.
533. 明槍易躲, 暗箭難防.
534. 你強困難弱, 你弱困難強.
535. 砌牆先打基, 吃蛋先養雞.
536. 牆倒眾人推.
537. 牆有縫, 壁有耳.
538. 強中自有強中手.
539. 一家砌牆, 兩家好看.
540. 巧者多勞拙者閒.
541. 勤勞益壽, 安逸亡身.
542. 勤是搖錢樹, 儉是聚寶盆.

543. 勤為無價寶，慎是護身符．

544. 勤以補拙．

545. 勤以致富．

546. 勤有功，嬉無益．

547. 人勤地生寶，人懶地生草．

548. 書山有路勤為徑．

549. 一勤生百巧，一懶生百病．

550. 遠親不如近鄰．

551. 只勤沒儉，有針沒線．

552. 情海無風，波浪自起．

553. 情人眼裡出西施．

554. 水火無情．

555. 窮不可欺，富不可恃．

556. 窮則變，變則通．

557. 窮則獨善其身，達則兼善天下．

558. 食不窮，穿不窮，不會打算一世窮．

559. 欲窮千里目，更上一層樓．

560. 人不求人一般大．

561. 人到無求品自高．

562. 曲高和寡.
563. 打人一拳, 防人一腳.
564. 百樣雀兒百樣音.
565. 得饒人處且饒人.
566. 熱極生風.
567. 己所不欲, 勿施於人.
568. 謀事在人, 成事在天.
569. 求人不如求己.
570. 人不在大小, 馬不在高低.
571. 人不知己醜, 馬不知臉長.
572. 人定勝天.
573. 人多嘴雜.
574. 人非草木, 孰能無情?
575. 人非聖賢, 孰能無過?
576. 人各有所好.
577. 人會變, 月會圓.
578. 人勤地不懶.
579. 人往高處爬, 水往低處流.
580. 人無廉恥, 百事可為.

581. 人在世上煉, 刀在石上磨.

582. 仁者見仁, 智者見智.

583. 忍字家中寶.

584. 生老病死, 人之常情.

585. 天不生無用之人, 地不長無名之草.

586. 推己及人.

587. 日光不照門, 醫生就上門.

588. 無事嫌日長, 有事嫌日短.

589. 柔能克剛.

590. 欺軟必怕硬.

591. 天下無不散的宴席.

592. 不塞不流, 不止不行.

593. 美色無美德, 好比花無香.

594. 聚沙成塔.

595. 快織無好紗, 快嫁無好家.

596. 沙粒雖小傷人眼.

597. 不上高山, 不顯平地.

598. 從善如登, 從惡如崩.

599. 積善者昌.

600. 積善之家,必有餘慶.
601. 江山易改,本性難移.
602. 靠山吃山,靠水吃水.
603. 來者不善,善者不來.
604. 留得青山在,不怕沒柴燒.
605. 人間到處有青山.
606. 人善被人欺,馬善被人騎.
607. 善不積,不足以成名.
608. 善始善終.
609. 善始則功近于成.
610. 上善若水.
611. 為善常樂.
612. 學善三年,學惡一朝.
613. 要知山中事,須問打柴人.
614. 一山難容二虎.
615. 有山必有路,有水必有渡.
616. 這山望著那山高.
617. 刀傷易治,口傷難醫.
618. 積少成多.

619. 少年不知勤學早, 白頭方悔讀書遲.
620. 少壯不努力, 老大徒傷悲.
621. 人心不足蛇吞象.
622. 舌長事長, 夜長夢多.
623. 舌劍利於刀劍.
624. 一朝被蛇咬, 十年怕草繩.
625. 不會燒香得罪神, 不會講話得罪人.
626. 健全之精神, 寓於健全之身體.
627. 寧可身冷, 不可心冷.
628. 求神不如求人.
629. 身教勝於言教.
630. 後生可畏.
631. 久賭無勝家.
632. 人非生而知之, 乃學而知之.
633. 人生七十才開始.
634. 人之生也柔弱, 其死也堅強.
635. 三天不唸口生, 三年不做手生.
636. 勝敗乃兵家常事.
637. 勝不驕, 敗不餒.

638. 生恩不如養恩.

639. 生有涯而知無涯.

640. 生於憂患, 死於安樂.

641. 一回生, 二回熟.

642. 一日省一把, 三年買瓜馬.

643. 不經一事, 不長一智.

644. 不怕事情難, 就怕不耐煩.

645. 管閒事, 落不是.

646. 滾石不生苔, 轉業不聚財.

647. 好事不出門, 壞事傳千里.

648. 好石磨刀也要水.

649. 今日事, 今日畢.

650. 失敗是成功之母.

651. 施比受有福.

652. 事成於和睦, 力生於團結.

653. 事非經過不知難.

654. 是非難逃眾口.

655. 是非終日有, 不聽自然無.

656. 是非自有公論.

657. 士可殺不可辱.

658. 事實勝於雄辯.

659. 識時務者為俊傑.

660. 時勢造英雄.

661. 事雖小, 不做不成; 子孫賢, 不教不明.

662. 他山之石, 可以攻錯.

663. 天下事豈能盡人意.

664. 嚴師出高徒.

665. 一家有事, 四鄰不安.

666. 以勢服人口, 以理服人心.

667. 有錢人怕事.

668. 欲遠是非, 慎交為先.

669. 只要苦幹, 事成一半.

670. 做事容易, 做人難.

671. 豐收沒有巧, 多鋤幾遍草.

672. 好手難繡沒線花.

673. 兩人養馬瘦, 兩人養船漏.

674. 七手八腳必敗事.

675. 巧手難使兩根針.

676. 勤快人用手，懶惰人用口．

677. 一分耕耘，一分收獲．

678. 大樹也有枯枝．

679. 好書不厭百回讀．

680. 沒有梧桐樹，那招鳳凰來．

681. 貧者因書而富，富者因書而貴．

682. 十年樹木，百年樹人．

683. 樹大招風．

684. 書到用時方恨少．

685. 書讀百遍，其義自明．

686. 樹高千丈，葉落歸根．

687. 樹老半心空，人老百事通．

688. 熟能生巧．

689. 樹怕剝皮，人怕傷心．

690. 樹小扶直易，樹大扶直難．

691. 無巧不成書．

692. 滴水穿石．

693. 肥水不落外人田．

694. 覆水難收．

695. 井水不犯河水.

696. 流水不腐, 戶樞不蠹.

697. 怕水當不了漁夫.

698. 水不流會臭, 苗不管沒收.

699. 水淺不容大舟.

700. 水深不響, 響水不深.

701. 水深流去慢, 智人話語遲.

702. 水雖平, 亦有波; 衡雖準, 亦有差.

703. 水至清則無魚.

704. 遠水救不了近火.

705. 遠水止不了近渴.

706. 早睡早起精神好.

707. 好人說不壞, 好酒攪不酸.

708. 路上說話, 草裡有人.

709. 說曹操, 曹操就到.

710. 寧可潔身而死, 不願污身而生.

711. 三思而後行.

712. 私中有過, 忙中有錯.

713. 欲速則不達.

714. 嫁雞隨雞, 嫁狗隨狗.

715. 歲月不饒人.

716. 歲月添人壽, 悲愁催人老.

717. 日月如梭.

718. 九層之台, 起于壘土.

719. 貪者必失.

720. 皇天不負苦心人.

721. 瞞天瞞地, 瞞不過鄰居.

722. 天不言自高, 地不言自厚.

723. 天才在於勤奮.

724. 天有不測風雲, 人有旦夕禍福.

725. 天有寒暑陰晴, 人有悲歡離合.

726. 天有好生之德.

727. 天助自助者.

728. 一朝天子, 一朝臣.

729. 有上不去的天, 沒有過不去的關.

730. 一人難調百味羹.

731. 眾口難調.

732. 打鐵先得本身硬.

733. 打鐵要趁熱.

734. 好鐵不打釘, 好男不當兵.

735. 冷鐵難打, 老竹難彎.

736. 會說不如會聽.

737. 空桶響叮噹

738. 十事半通, 不如一藝精通.

739. 同聲相應, 同氣相求.

740. 爲人不當頭, 爲木不當軸.

741. 狡兔有三窟.

742. 善惡不同途.

743. 萬物生於土, 萬物歸於土.

744. 一逐二兔, 一兔不得.

745. 團結就是力量.

746. 團結力量大, 柴多火焰高.

747. 團結一條心, 黃土變黃金.

748. 觀其外而知其內.

749. 人外有人, 山外有山.

750. 端人家碗, 服人家管.

751. 萬事起頭難.

752. 一隻碗不響, 兩隻碗叮噹.

753. 天網恢恢, 疏而不漏.

754. 審其為人, 觀其諸友.

755. 百聞不如一見.

756. 不知就問, 不能則學.

757. 耳聞為虛, 眼見為實.

758. 怕問路, 要迷路.

759. 問遍萬家成行家.

760. 穩健紮實必致勝.

761. 問路不施禮, 多走二十里.

762. 自家的文章, 人家的婆娘.

763. 強記不如善悟.

764. 天下烏鴉一般黑.

765. 物極必反.

766. 烏鴉報喜沒人信.

767. 烏鴉不與鳳凰棲.

768. 物要防爛, 人要防懶.

769. 物以類聚.

770. 物以稀為貴.

771. 一物降一物.

772. 悲喜為鄰.

773. 娶個媳婦分個家.

774. 娶了媳婦忘了娘.

775. 人逢喜事精神爽.

776. 文戲靠嘴, 武戲靠腿.

777. 習慣成自然.

778. 一代好媳婦, 三代好兒孫.

779. 先下手為強, 後下手遭殃.

780. 單絲不成線.

781. 放長線, 釣大魚.

782. 人閒生病, 石閒生苔.

783. 小人閒居做歹事.

784. 不怕箱櫃空, 只要有個好老公.

785. 你養我小, 我養你老.

786. 人無笑臉不開店.

787. 五十步笑百步.

788. 小不忍則亂大謀.

789. 小孩不能慣, 一慣定有亂.

790. 小孩嘴裡吐真言.
791. 笑口常開, 青春常在.
792. 笑門開, 幸福來.
793. 小人得寸便進尺.
794. 小人記仇, 君子感恩.
795. 小人心多, 矮樹根多.
796. 小人自大, 小溪聲大.
797. 小時不知老娘親, 育兒才知報娘恩.
798. 小時了了, 大未必佳.
799. 小時偷針, 大了偷金.
800. 小心駛得萬年船.
801. 小心天下可走, 鹵莽寸步難行.
802. 一笑治百病.
803. 好鞋不踩臭狗屎.
804. 害人之心不可有, 防人之心不可無.
805. 交人交心, 澆花澆根.
806. 盡信書不如不讀書.
807. 勞心者治人, 勞力者治於人.
808. 女人心, 海底針.

809. 人而無信, 不知其可?

810. 人同心, 土變金.

811. 人心高過天, 做了皇帝想成仙.

812. 人心難摸.

813. 人心要公, 火心要空.

814. 三人同心奪天下.

815. 心歡返少年.

816. 心寬體胖.

817. 心裡痛快百病消.

818. 心中有誰, 誰就漂亮.

819. 一心不能二用.

820. 多行不義必目斃.

821. 夫妻和, 家務興; 夫妻不和, 睡不寧.

822. 千里之行, 始於足下.

823. 三人行必有我師.

824. 熟水性, 好划船.

825. 聞雞起舞, 百事俱興.

826. 行百里者半九十.

827. 行動勝於空談.

828. 親兄弟, 明算帳.
829. 兄弟不知鄰里欺, 將相不睦鄰國欺.
830. 兄弟不知硬過鐵.
831. 兄弟鬩于牆, 外御其侮.
832. 不為不知而羞, 要為不學而愧.
833. 秀才不出門, 能知天下事.
834. 秀才餓死不賣書, 壯士窮死不賣藝.
835. 千虛不如一實.
836. 循序漸進, 無業不成.
837. 一人傳虛, 萬人傳實.
838. 邊學邊問, 才有學問.
839. 不入虎穴, 焉得虎子.
840. 各人自掃門前雪, 莫管他人瓦上霜.
841. 跟什麼人學什麼樣, 跟著屠夫學不成皮匠.
842. 人不學, 不知義.
843. 學不厭老.
844. 學不知謙, 藝必有限.
845. 學而不思則罔, 思而不學則殆.

846. 學怕一知半解, 飯怕半生不熟.

847. 學如逆水行舟, 不進則退.

848. 學無老少, 能者為師.

849. 學無止境.

850. 學習如趕路, 不能歇一步.

851. 會選的選兒郎, 不會選的選家當.

852. 不聽老人言, 吃苦在眼前.

853. 多言惹禍.

854. 紅顏多薄命.

855. 緊睜眼, 慢張口.

856. 快人一言, 快馬一鞭.

857. 良言入耳三冬暖, 惡言傷人六月寒.

858. 巧言令色鮮于仁.

859. 人在矮簷下, 不可不低頭.

860. 言必信, 行必果.

861. 眼不見為淨.

862. 眼不見, 心不煩.

863. 言多必失.

864. 嚴是愛, 鬆是害, 不管不教要變壞.

865. 眼斜心不正, 鼻歪竟不端.

866. 嚴以律己, 寬以待人.

867. 一言既出, 駟馬難追.

868. 亡羊補牢, 猶未爲晚.

869. 樣樣通, 樣樣鬆.

870. 對症下藥, 藥到病除.

871. 良藥苦口, 忠言逆耳.

872. 藥補不如食補.

873. 創業難, 守成更難.

814. 千秋大業, 非一日之功.

815. 業精于勤, 荒于嬉.

816. 不怕人不請, 就怕藝不精.

817. 見義思遷業難成.

818. 借來的衣裳不合體.

879. 開卷有益.

880. 民意不可侮.

881. 鳥貴有翼, 人貴有志.

882. 藝高人膽大.

883. 疑人莫用, 用人莫疑.

884. 衣裳長了絆腿，心眼多了受累．

885. 疑心生暗鬼．

886. 一藝傍身，終身受用．

887. 單弦不成音．

888. 姻緣可遇不可求．

889. 姻緣天註定．

890. 不以成敗論英雄．

891. 英雄不怕出身低．

892. 英雄難過美人關．

893. 英雄所見略同．

894. 英雄有淚不輕彈．

895. 制服猛虎非英雄，抑住脾氣真好漢．

896. 故友勝新知．

897. 交友分厚薄，穿衣看寒暑．

848. 人到中年萬事憂．

899. 憂鬱七身．

900. 百日連陰雨，總有一朝晴．

901. 池裏無魚蝦爲大，山中無虎猴爲王．

902. 春雨貴如油．

903. 凡事預則立, 不預則廢.

904. 積羽沉舟.

905. 寧爲玉碎, 不爲瓦全.

906. 貪食魚兒易上鈎.

907. 未雨綢繆.

908. 小雨久下能成災.

909. 雨不能下一年, 人不能窮一輩.

910. 玉不琢, 不成器.

911. 預防勝於治療.

912. 愚者千慮, 必有一得.

913. 抓魚要下水, 伐木要入林.

914. 不是冤家不聚頭.

915. 寧走十步遠, 不走一步險.

916. 行遠必自邇.

917. 飲水要思源, 爲人不忘本.

918. 有緣千里來相會, 無緣對面不相識.

919. 冤仇宜解不宜結.

920. 遠處著眼, 近處著手.

921. 冤家路窄.

922. 冤有頭, 債有主.

923. 獨樂樂, 不如眾樂樂.

924. 日中則昃, 月盈則食.

925. 月兒彎彎照九州, 幾家歡樂幾家愁.

926. 天下無雲不下雨, 世間無理事不成.

927. 雲不聚集雨不下, 人不團結力不大.

928. 欠債的多健忘, 討債的記性強.

929. 做賊越老越膽小.

930. 無債一身輕.

931. 人要長交, 賬要短結.

932. 一着不慎, 滿盤皆輸.

933. 臨陣磨刀晚.

934. 無針不引線, 無水不行船.

935. 興家猶如針挑土, 敗家好似水推舟.

936. 一針不補, 千針難縫.

937. 一枝針無兩頭利.

938. 只要功夫深, 鐵杵磨成針.

939. 己身正, 不令而行.

940. 理正不怕法.

941. 人爭一口氣, 佛爭一炷香.

942. 身正不怕影兒斜.

943. 心不正, 行不穩.

944. 心正不怕邪.

945. 疑人心不正, 心正不疑人.

946. 一爭兩醜, 一讓兩有.

947. 鷸蚌相爭, 漁翁得利.

948. 不怕知短, 就怕老短.

949. 船到橋頭自然直.

950. 大智若愚.

951. 好漢憑老強, 好馬憑膽壯.

952. 撿了芝麻, 丟了西瓜.

953. 人貴有老, 學貴有恆.

954. 人憑老氣虎憑威.

955. 人窮老短.

956. 人生無老, 如無舵之舟.

957. 人有老, 竹有節.

958. 人之相知, 貴在知心.

959. 若要人不知, 除非己莫為.

960. 小蹟防大跌.

961. 有志不在年高.

962. 有志婦人勝過男子.

963. 有志飄風洋過海, 無志寸步難行.

964. 有志者事竟成.

965. 欲知心腹事, 先聽口中言.

966. 紙包不住火.

967. 知己知彼, 百戰百勝.

968. 知識就是力量.

969. 知識愈淺, 自信愈深.

970. 知者不言, 言者不知.

971. 智者寡言, 愚者多嘴.

972. 智者千慮, 必有一失.

973. 知之為知之, 不知為不知, 是知也.

974. 蜘蛛勤織網, 總有飛來蟲.

975. 蜘蛛張網好天氣.

976. 不摸秤桿, 不知砣重.

977. 將相本無種, 男兒當自強.

978. 重為輕根.

979. 腐木不可為柱, 卑人不可為主.

980. 好竹出好筍.

981. 近朱者赤, 近墨者黑.

982. 一根柱子動, 根根尾梁搖.

983. 遠住香, 近住涼.

984. 猪多肉賤.

985. 人心專, 石山穿.

986. 骨體壯人欺病, 骨體弱人病欺.

987. 教子從小起, 治家勤儉起.

988. 少吃多滋味, 多吃活受罪.

989. 賜子千金, 不如賜子一藝.

990. 縱兒害兒, 縱妻害自己.

991. 捷足先登.

992. 一失足成千古恨.

993. 衣食足則知榮辱.

994. 知足常樂.

995. 狗嘴吐不出象牙.

996. 忍嘴不欠債.

997. 人嘴如青草, 風吹兩邊倒.

998. 嘴巧奪上風.
999. 寧可做過, 不可錯過.
1000. 坐吃山空.

DICTIONARY OF 1,000 JEWISH PROVERBS
David C. Gross
Jewish proverbs, ancient and contemporary, encompass a wide range of subjects, reflecting lives that were often impoverished materially but rich spiritually. These old and new proverbs became part of the Jewish people's heritage and were not only passed on through the generations, but also expanded upon continually. The one thousand proverbs offered here are arranged by Hebrew subject, followed by a transliteration into English from either Hebrew, Yiddish, or Aramaic followed then by an English translation. For easy reference, a complete English index of the subjects appears at the back of the book.
131 pp • 5 ½ x 8 ½ • 0-7818-0529-5 • W • $11.95pb • (628)

DICTIONARY OF 1,000 POLISH PROVERBS
131 pp • 5 ½ x 8 ½ • 0-7818-0482-5 • W • $11.95pb • (628)

A TREASURY OF POLISH APHORISMS, A Bilingual Edition
Compiled and translated by Jacek Galazka
Twenty years ago *Unkempt Thoughts*, a collection of Polish aphorisms by Stanislaw Jerzy Lec was published in English and became an instant success. Clifton Fadiman called Lec: "one of the remarkable wits of our dark time, eminently attuned to it." A selection of his aphorisms opens this collection, which comprises 225 aphorisms by eighty Polish writers, many of them well known in their native land. A selection of thirty Polish proverbs is included representing some uniquely Polish expressions of universal wisdom. These were translated by Helen Stankiewicz Zand, a noted translator of Polish fiction. Twenty pen and ink drawings by a talented Polish illustrator Barbara Swidzinska complete this remarkable exploration of true Polish wit and wisdom.
140 pp • 5 ½ x 8 ½ • 20 illustrations • 0-7818-0549-X • W • $12.95 • (647)

COMPREHENSIVE BILINGUAL DICTIONARY OF RUSSIAN PROVERBS
edited by Peter Mertvago
477 pp • 8 ½ x 11 • 5,335 entries, index • 0-7818-0424-8 • $35.00pb • (555)

DICTIONARY OF 1,000 RUSSIAN PROVERBS
130 pp 5 ½ x 8 ½ 0-7818-0564-3 W $11.95pb (694)

DICTIONARY OF 1,000 SPANISH PROVERBS
131 pp • 5 ½ x 8 ½ • bilingual • 0-7818-0412-4 • W • $11.95pb • (254)

A CLASSIFIED COLLECTION OF TAMIL PROVERBS
edited by Rev. Herman Jensen
499 pp • 3,644 entries • 0-7818-0592-9 • 19.95pb • (699)

Dictionaries

CAMBODIAN-ENGLISH/ENGLISH-CAMBODIAN STANDARD DICTIONARY
355 pp • 5 ½ x 8 ¼ • 15,000 entries • 0-87052-818-1 • NA • $8.95pb • (451)

CHINESE HANDY DICTIONARY
120 pp • 5 x 7 ¾ • 0-87052-050-4 • USA • $8.95pb • (347)

CLASSIFIED AND ILLUSTRATED CHINESE-ENGLISH DICTIONARY, Revised
897 pp • 5 ¼ x 7 ½ • 35,000 entries • 2,000 illust • 0-87052-714-2 • NA • $19.95hc • (27)

ENGLISH-CHINESE (PINYIN) DICTIONARY
500 pp • 4 x 6 • 10,000 entries • 0-7818-0427-2 • $19.95pb • USA • (509)

JAPANESE-ENGLISH/ENGLISH-JAPANESE CONCISE DICTIONARY, Romanized
235 pp • 4 x 6 • 8,000 entries • 0-7818-0162-1 • W • $11.95pb • (474)

JAPANESE HANDY DICTIONARY
120 pp • 5 x 7 ¾ • 0-87052-962-5 • $8.95pb • NA • (466)

KOREAN-ENGLISH/ENGLISH-KOREAN PRACTICAL DICTIONARY
365 pp • 4 x 7¼ • 8,500 entries • 0-87052-092-X • Asia and NA • $14.95pb • (399)

KOREAN HANDY DICTIONARY
186 pp • 5 x 7 ¾ • 0-7818-0082-X • W • $8.95pb • (438)

THAI HANDY DICTIONARY
120 pp • 5 x 7 ¾ • 0-87052-963-3 • USA • $8.95pb • (468)

Tutorial
CANTONESE BASIC COURSE
416 pp • 5 ½ x 8 ½ • 0-7818-0289-X • W • $19.95pb • (117)

BEGINNER'S CHINESE
150 pp • 5 ½ x 8 • 0-7818-0566-X • $14.95pb • W • (690)

MASTERING JAPANESE
368 pp • 5 ½ x 8 ½ • 0-87052-923-4 • USA • $14.95pb • (523)
2 Cassettes: • 0-87052-983-8 USA • $12.95 • (524)

BEGINNER'S JAPANESE
200 pp • 5 ½ x 8 ½ • 0-7818-0234-2 • W • $11.95pb • (53)

LAO BASIC COURSE
350 pp • 5 ½ x 8¼ • 0-7818-0410-8 • W • $19.95pb • (470)

BEGINNER'S VIETNAMESE
517 pp • 7 x 10 • 30 lessons • 0-7818-0411-6 • $19.95pb • W • (253)

Cookbooks
THE JOY OF CHINESE COOKING
Doreen Yen Hung Feng
Includes over two hundred kitchen-tested recipes, detailed illustrations and a
thorough index.
226 pp • 5 ½ x 7 ½ • 0-7818-0097-8 • $8.95pb • (288)

<u>History</u>
KOREA: THE FIRST WAR WE LOST, REVISED EDITION
Bevin Alexander
This bestselling account of the Korean War has now been updated with two additional chapters.
"Well researched and readable."   —*The New York Times*
"This is arguably the most reliable and fully-realized one volume history of the Korean War since David Rees' *Korea.*"—*Publisher's Weekly*
"Bevin Alexander does a superb job . . .this respectable and fast-moving study is the first to be written by a professional army historian."   —*Library Journal*

Bevin Alexander is a noted journalist who was a combat historian during the Korean War, commander of the 5th Historical Detachment and author of numerous battle studies for the U.S. Army. He resides in Bremo Bluff, Virginia.
580 pp • 13 maps, index • 6 x 9 • 0-7818-0577-5 • W • $19.95pb

AUSTRALIAN DICTIONARY AND PHRASEBOOK
131 pp • 4 3 ¾ x 7 • 1,500 entries • 0-7818-0539-2 • W • $11.95pb • (626)

BASQUE-ENGLISH/ ENGLISH-BASQUE DICTIONARY AND
PHRASEBOOK
240 pages • 3 ¾ x 7 • 1,500 entries • 0-7818-0622-4 • W • $11.95pb (751)

BOSNIAN-ENGLISH/ENGLISH-BOSNIAN DICTIONARY AND
PHRASEBOOK
175 pp • 3 ¾ x 7 • 1,500 entries • 0-7818-0596-1 • W • $11.95pb • (691)

BRETON-ENGLISH/ENGLISH-BRETON DICTIONARY AND
PHRASEBOOK
131 pp • 3 ¾ x 7 • 1,500 entries • 0-7818-0540-6 • W • $11.95pb • (627)

BRITISH-AMERICAN/AMERICAN-BRITISH DICTIONARY AND
PHRASEBOOK
160 pp • 3 ¾ x 7 • 1,400 entries • 0-7818-0450-7 • W • $11.95pb • (247)

CHECHEN-ENGLISH/ENGLISH-CHECHEN DICTIONARY AND
PHRASEBOOK
160 pp • 3 ¾ x 7 • 1,400 entries • 0-7818-0446-9 • NA • $11.95pb • (183)

GEORGIAN-ENGLISH/ENGLISH-GEORGIAN DICTIONARY AND
PHRASEBOOK
150 pp • 3 ¾ x 7 • 1,300 entries • 0-7818-0542-2 • W • $11.95pb • (630)

GREEK-ENGLISH/ ENGLISH-GREEK DICTIONARY AND
PHRASEBOOK
175 pages • 3 ¾ x 7 • 1,500 entries • 0-7818-0635-6 • W • $11.95pb • (715)

IRISH-ENGLISH/ENGLISH-IRISH DICTIONARY AND PHRASEBOOK
160 pp • 3 ¾ x 7 • 1,400 entries/phrases • 0-87052-110-1 NA • $7.95pb • (385)

LINGALA-ENGLISH/ENGLISH-LINGALA DICTIONARY AND
PHRASEBOOK
120 pp • 3 ¾ x 7 • 0-7818-0456-6 • W • $11.95pb • (296)

MALTESE-ENGLISH/ENGLISH-MALTESE DICTIONARY AND
PHRASEBOOK
175 pp 3 ¾ x 7 • 1,500 entries • 0-7818-0565-1 • W • $11.95pb • (697)

POLISH DICTIONARY AND PHRASEBOOK
252 pp • 5 ½ x 8 ½ • 0-7818-0134-6 • W • $11.95pb • (192)
Cassettes—Vol I: 0-7818-0340-3 • W • $12.95 • (492); Vol II: 0-7818-0384-5 • W • $12.95 • (486)

RUSSIAN DICTIONARY AND PHRASEBOOK, Revised
256pp • 5 ½ x 8 ½ • 3,000 entries • 0-7818-0190-7 • W • $9.95pb • (597)

UKRAINIAN DICTIONARY AND PHRASEBOOK
205pp • 5 ½ X 8 ½ • 3,000 entries • 0-7818-0188-5 • w • $11.95pb • (28)

Practical Dictionaries From Hippocrene:

AFRIKAANS-ENGLISH/ ENGLISH AFRIKAANS PRACTICAL DICTIONARY
430 pages • $1/2 x 6 ½ • 14,000 entries • 0-7818-0052-8 • NA • (134)

ALBANIAN-ENGLISH/ ENGLISH-ALBANIAN PRACTICAL DICTIONARY
400 pages • 4 3/8 x 7 • 18,000 entries • 0-7818-0419-1 • W except Albania • $14.95pb • (483)

BULGARIAN-ENGLISH/ ENGLISH-BULGARIAN PRACTICAL DICTIONARY
323 pages • 4 3/8 x 7 • 6,500 entries • 0-87052-145-4 • NA • $14.95pb • (331)

DANISH-ENGLISH/ ENGLISH-DANISH PRACTICAL DICTIONARY
601 pages • 4 3/8 x 7 • 32,000 entries • 0-7818-0823-8 • NA • $14.95pb • (198)

FRENCH-ENGLISH/ ENGLISH-FRENCH PRACTICAL DICTIONARY, with larger print
386 pages • 5 ½ x 8 ¼ • 35,00 entries • 0-7818-0355-1 • W • $9.95pb • (499)

FULANI-ENGLISH PRACTICAL DICTIONARY
264 pages • 5 x 7 ¼ • 0-7818-0404-3 • W • $14.95pb • (38)

GERMAN-ENGLISH/ ENGLISH-GERMAN PRACTICAL DICTIONARY, with larger print
400 pages • 5 ½ x 8 ¼ • 35,000 entries • 0-7818-0355-1 • W • $9.95pb • (200)

HINDI-ENGLISH/ ENGLISH-HINDI PRACTICAL DICTIONARY
745 pages • 4 3/8 x 7 • 25,000 entries • 0-7818-0084-6 • W • $19.95pb • (442)

ENGLISH-HINDI PRACTICAL DICTIONARY
399 pages • 4 3/8 x 7 • 15,000 entries • 0-87052-978-1 • NA • $11.95pb • (362)

INDIONESIAN-ENGLISH/ ENGLISH-INDONESIAN PRACTICAL DICTIONARY
289 pages • 4 ¼ x 7 • 17,000 entries • 0-87052-810-6 • NA • $11.95pb • (127)

ITALIAN -ENGLISH/ ENGLISH-ITALIAN PRACTICAL DICTIONARY, with larger print
488 pages • 5 ½ x 8 ¼ • 35,000 entries • 0-7818-0354-3 • W • $9.95p • (201)

KOREAN-ENGLISH/ ENGLISH KOREAN PRACTICAL DICTIONARY
365 pages • 4 x 7 ¼ • 8,500 entries • 0-87052-092-x • Asia and NA • 414.95pb • (399)

LATVIAN-ENGLISH/ ENGLISH-LATVIAN PRACTICAL DICTIONARY
474 pages • 4 3/8 x 7 • 16,000 entries • 0-7818-0059-5 • NA • $16.95pb • (194)

POLISH-ENGLISH/ ENGLISH-POLISH PRACTICAL DICTIONARY
703 pages • 5 ¼ x 8 ½ • 31,000 entries • 0-7818-0085-4 • W • $11.95pb • (450)

SERBO-CROATIAN-ENGLISH/ ENGLISH-SERBO-CROATIAN PRACTICAL DICTIO-NARY
400 pages • 5 3/8 x 7 • 24,000 entries • 0-7818-0445-0 • W • $16.95pb • (130)

UKRAINIAN-ENGLISH/ ENGLISH-UKRAINIAN PRACTICAL DICTIO-NARY, Revised edition with menu terms
406 pages • 41/4 x 7 • 16,000 entries • 0-7818-0306-3 • W • $14.95pb • (343)

YIDDISH-ENGLISH/ ENGLISH-YIDDISH PRACTICAL DICTIONARY, Expanded edition
215 pages • 4 ½ x 7 • 4,000 entries • 0-7818-0439-6 • W • $9.95pb • (431)

All prices are subject to change. To order Hippocrene Books, contact your local bookstore, call (718) 454-2366, or write to : Hippocrene Books, 171 Madison Ave. New York, NY 10016. Please enclose check or money order adding $5.00 shipping (UPS) for the first book and $.50 for each additional title.